WILD CAMPING
6"x9" 120 Pages

Camping Equipment Check List

Tent □ Fly-sheet □ Tent poles □ Ground sheet □ Bed roll □
Sleeping bag □ Pillow □ Tent pegs □ Rope □ Mallet □
Water container □ Lantern/torch □ Camping Gaz □
Matches □ Lighter □ Insect repellent □ Pans □ Money □
Portable shovel □ Plates □ Knives and forks □ Clothing □
Camping Knife □ Rucksack □ Food Items □ Mobile Phone □
Mobile phone charger □ Solar charger □ Map □ Pen □
Water Purifying tablets □ First Aid Kit □ Binoculars □

Location of nearest Town/Village:

_____

Mode of transport? Foot □ Bike □ Motorbike □ Car □

Location of landowner/farm:_____

Permission obtained to camp here? Y □ N □

Date: ____/____/_____

Expected Duration of stay? 1 □ 2 □ 3 □ 4 □ 5 □ Nights

How was the stay?_____

Any problems? _____

Notes:

Camping Equipment Check List

Tent □ Fly-sheet □ Tent poles □ Ground sheet □ Bed roll □

Sleeping bag □ Pillow □ Tent pegs □ Rope □ Mallet □

Water container □ Lantern/torch □ Camping Gaz □

Matches □ Lighter □ Insect repellent □ Pans □ Money □

Portable shovel □ Plates □ Knives and forks □ Clothing □

Camping Knife □ Rucksack □ Food Items □ Mobile Phone □

Mobile phone charger □ Solar charger □ Map □ Pen □

Water Purifying tablets □ First Aid Kit □ Binoculars □

Location of nearest Town/Village:

_____

Mode of transport? Foot □ Bike □ Motorbike □ Car □

Location of landowner/farm:_____

Permission obtained to camp here? Y □ N □

Date: _____/_____/_____

Expected Duration of stay? 1 □ 2 □ 3 □ 4 □ 5 □ Nights

 How was the stay?_____

 Any problems? _____

Notes:

Camping Equipment Check List

Tent □ Fly-sheet □ Tent poles □ Ground sheet □ Bed roll □

Sleeping bag □ Pillow □ Tent pegs □ Rope □ Mallet □

Water container □ Lantern/torch □ Camping Gaz □

Matches □ Lighter □ Insect repellent □ Pans □ Money □

Portable shovel □ Plates □ Knives and forks □ Clothing □

Camping Knife □ Rucksack □ Food Items □ Mobile Phone □

Mobile phone charger □ Solar charger □ Map □ Pen □

Water Purifying tablets □ First Aid Kit □ Binoculars □

Location of nearest Town/Village:

_____

Mode of transport? Foot □ Bike □ Motorbike □ Car □

Location of landowner/farm:_____

Permission obtained to camp here? Y □ N □

Date: ____/____/_____

Expected Duration of stay? 1 □ 2 □ 3 □ 4 □ 5 □ Nights

 How was the stay?_____

 Any problems? _____

Notes:

Camping Equipment Check List

Tent □ Fly-sheet □ Tent poles □ Ground sheet □ Bed roll □
Sleeping bag □ Pillow □ Tent pegs □ Rope □ Mallet □
Water container □ Lantern/torch □ Camping Gaz □
Matches □ Lighter □ Insect repellent □ Pans □ Money □
Portable shovel □ Plates □ Knives and forks □ Clothing □
Camping Knife □ Rucksack □ Food Items □ Mobile Phone □
Mobile phone charger □ Solar charger □ Map □ Pen □
Water Purifying tablets □ First Aid Kit □ Binoculars □

Location of nearest Town/Village:
_____

Mode of transport? Foot □ Bike □ Motorbike □ Car □
Location of landowner/farm:_____
Permission obtained to camp here? Y □ N □
Date: ____/____/_____
Expected Duration of stay? 1 □ 2 □ 3 □ 4 □ 5 □ Nights
 How was the stay?_____
 Any problems? _____
Notes:

Camping Equipment Check List

Tent □ Fly-sheet □ Tent poles □ Ground sheet □ Bed roll □
Sleeping bag □ Pillow □ Tent pegs □ Rope □ Mallet □
Water container □ Lantern/torch □ Camping Gaz □
Matches □ Lighter □ Insect repellent □ Pans □ Money □
Portable shovel □ Plates □ Knives and forks □ Clothing □
Camping Knife □ Rucksack □ Food Items □ Mobile Phone □
Mobile phone charger □ Solar charger □ Map □ Pen □
Water Purifying tablets □ First Aid Kit □ Binoculars □

Location of nearest Town/Village:

_____

Mode of transport? Foot □ Bike □ Motorbike □ Car □

Location of landowner/farm:_____

Permission obtained to camp here? Y □ N □

Date: ____/____/_____

Expected Duration of stay? 1 □ 2 □ 3 □ 4 □ 5 □ Nights

 How was the stay?_____

 Any problems? _____

Notes:

Camping Equipment Check List

Tent □ Fly-sheet □ Tent poles □ Ground sheet □ Bed roll □

Sleeping bag □ Pillow □ Tent pegs □ Rope □ Mallet □

Water container □ Lantern/torch □ Camping Gaz □

Matches □ Lighter □ Insect repellent □ Pans □ Money □

Portable shovel □ Plates □ Knives and forks □ Clothing □

Camping Knife □ Rucksack □ Food Items □ Mobile Phone □

Mobile phone charger □ Solar charger □ Map □ Pen □

Water Purifying tablets □ First Aid Kit □ Binoculars □

Location of nearest Town/Village:

_____

Mode of transport? Foot □ Bike □ Motorbike □ Car □

Location of landowner/farm:_____

Permission obtained to camp here? Y □ N □

Date: ____/____/_____

Expected Duration of stay? 1 □ 2 □ 3 □ 4 □ 5 □ Nights

How was the stay?_____

Any problems? _____

Notes:

Camping Equipment Check List

Tent □ Fly-sheet □ Tent poles □ Ground sheet □ Bed roll □
Sleeping bag □ Pillow □ Tent pegs □ Rope □ Mallet □
Water container □ Lantern/torch □ Camping Gaz □
Matches □ Lighter □ Insect repellent □ Pans □ Money □
Portable shovel □ Plates □ Knives and forks □ Clothing □
Camping Knife □ Rucksack □ Food Items □ Mobile Phone □
Mobile phone charger □ Solar charger □ Map □ Pen □
Water Purifying tablets □ First Aid Kit □ Binoculars □

Location of nearest Town/Village:

_____

Mode of transport? Foot □ Bike □ Motorbike □ Car □

Location of landowner/farm:_____

Permission obtained to camp here? Y □ N □

Date: ____/____/_____

Expected Duration of stay? 1 □ 2 □ 3 □ 4 □ 5 □ Nights

 How was the stay?_____

 Any problems? _____

Notes:

Camping Equipment Check List

Tent □ Fly-sheet □ Tent poles □ Ground sheet □ Bed roll □

Sleeping bag □ Pillow □ Tent pegs □ Rope □ Mallet □

Water container □ Lantern/torch □ Camping Gaz □

Matches □ Lighter □ Insect repellent □ Pans □ Money □

Portable shovel □ Plates □ Knives and forks □ Clothing □

Camping Knife □ Rucksack □ Food Items □ Mobile Phone □

Mobile phone charger □ Solar charger □ Map □ Pen □

Water Purifying tablets □ First Aid Kit □ Binoculars □

Location of nearest Town/Village:

_____

Mode of transport? Foot □ Bike □ Motorbike □ Car □

Location of landowner/farm:_____

Permission obtained to camp here? Y □ N □

Date: ____/____/_____

Expected Duration of stay? 1 □ 2 □ 3 □ 4 □ 5 □ Nights

How was the stay?_____

Any problems? _____

Notes:

Camping Equipment Check List

Tent □ Fly-sheet □ Tent poles □ Ground sheet □ Bed roll □

Sleeping bag □ Pillow □ Tent pegs □ Rope □ Mallet □

Water container □ Lantern/torch □ Camping Gaz □

Matches □ Lighter □ Insect repellent □ Pans □ Money □

Portable shovel □ Plates □ Knives and forks □ Clothing □

Camping Knife □ Rucksack □ Food Items □ Mobile Phone □

Mobile phone charger □ Solar charger □ Map □ Pen □

Water Purifying tablets □ First Aid Kit □ Binoculars □

Location of nearest Town/Village:

_____

Mode of transport? Foot □ Bike □ Motorbike □ Car □

Location of landowner/farm:_____

Permission obtained to camp here? Y □ N □

Date: ____/____/_____

Expected Duration of stay? 1 □ 2 □ 3 □ 4 □ 5 □ Nights

How was the stay?_____

Any problems? _____

Notes:

Camping Equipment Check List

Tent □ Fly-sheet □ Tent poles □ Ground sheet □ Bed roll □
Sleeping bag □ Pillow □ Tent pegs □ Rope □ Mallet □
Water container □ Lantern/torch □ Camping Gaz □
Matches □ Lighter □ Insect repellent □ Pans □ Money □
Portable shovel □ Plates □ Knives and forks □ Clothing □
Camping Knife □ Rucksack □ Food Items □ Mobile Phone □
Mobile phone charger □ Solar charger □ Map □ Pen □
Water Purifying tablets □ First Aid Kit □ Binoculars □

Location of nearest Town/Village:

_____

Mode of transport? Foot □ Bike □ Motorbike □ Car □
Location of landowner/farm:_____
Permission obtained to camp here? Y □ N □
Date: ____/____/_____
Expected Duration of stay? 1 □ 2 □ 3 □ 4 □ 5 □ Nights
 How was the stay?_____
 Any problems? _____
Notes:

Camping Equipment Check List

Tent □ Fly-sheet □ Tent poles □ Ground sheet □ Bed roll □

Sleeping bag □ Pillow □ Tent pegs □ Rope □ Mallet □

Water container □ Lantern/torch □ Camping Gaz □

Matches □ Lighter □ Insect repellent □ Pans □ Money □

Portable shovel □ Plates □ Knives and forks □ Clothing □

Camping Knife □ Rucksack □ Food Items □ Mobile Phone □

Mobile phone charger □ Solar charger □ Map □ Pen □

Water Purifying tablets □ First Aid Kit □ Binoculars □

Location of nearest Town/Village:

_____

Mode of transport? Foot □ Bike □ Motorbike □ Car □

Location of landowner/farm:_____

Permission obtained to camp here? Y □ N □

Date: ____/____/_____

Expected Duration of stay? 1 □ 2 □ 3 □ 4 □ 5 □ Nights

 How was the stay?_____

 Any problems? _____

Notes:

Camping Equipment Check List

Tent □ Fly-sheet □ Tent poles □ Ground sheet □ Bed roll □
Sleeping bag □ Pillow □ Tent pegs □ Rope □ Mallet □
Water container □ Lantern/torch □ Camping Gaz □
Matches □ Lighter □ Insect repellent □ Pans □ Money □
Portable shovel □ Plates □ Knives and forks □ Clothing □
Camping Knife □ Rucksack □ Food Items □ Mobile Phone □
Mobile phone charger □ Solar charger □ Map □ Pen □
Water Purifying tablets □ First Aid Kit □ Binoculars □

Location of nearest Town/Village:

_____

Mode of transport? Foot □ Bike □ Motorbike □ Car □
Location of landowner/farm:_____
Permission obtained to camp here? Y □ N □
Date: ____/____/_____
Expected Duration of stay? 1 □ 2 □ 3 □ 4 □ 5 □ Nights
 How was the stay?_____
 Any problems? _____
Notes:

Camping Equipment Check List

Tent □ Fly-sheet □ Tent poles □ Ground sheet □ Bed roll □
Sleeping bag □ Pillow □ Tent pegs □ Rope □ Mallet □
Water container □ Lantern/torch □ Camping Gaz □
Matches □ Lighter □ Insect repellent □ Pans □ Money □
Portable shovel □ Plates □ Knives and forks □ Clothing □
Camping Knife □ Rucksack □ Food Items □ Mobile Phone □
Mobile phone charger □ Solar charger □ Map □ Pen □
Water Purifying tablets □ First Aid Kit □ Binoculars □

Location of nearest Town/Village:

_____

Mode of transport? Foot □ Bike □ Motorbike □ Car □
Location of landowner/farm:_____
Permission obtained to camp here? Y □ N □
Date: ____/____/_____
Expected Duration of stay? 1 □ 2 □ 3 □ 4 □ 5 □ Nights
 How was the stay?_____
 Any problems? _____
Notes:

Camping Equipment Check List

Tent □ Fly-sheet □ Tent poles □ Ground sheet □ Bed roll □

Sleeping bag □ Pillow □ Tent pegs □ Rope □ Mallet □

Water container □ Lantern/torch □ Camping Gaz □

Matches □ Lighter □ Insect repellent □ Pans □ Money □

Portable shovel □ Plates □ Knives and forks □ Clothing □

Camping Knife □ Rucksack □ Food Items □ Mobile Phone □

Mobile phone charger □ Solar charger □ Map □ Pen □

Water Purifying tablets □ First Aid Kit □ Binoculars □

Location of nearest Town/Village:

_____

Mode of transport? Foot □ Bike □ Motorbike □ Car □

Location of landowner/farm:_____

Permission obtained to camp here? Y □ N □

Date: ____/____/_____

Expected Duration of stay? 1 □ 2 □ 3 □ 4 □ 5 □ Nights

How was the stay?_____

Any problems? _____

Notes:

Camping Equipment Check List

Tent □ Fly-sheet □ Tent poles □ Ground sheet □ Bed roll □

Sleeping bag □ Pillow □ Tent pegs □ Rope □ Mallet □

Water container □ Lantern/torch □ Camping Gaz □

Matches □ Lighter □ Insect repellent □ Pans □ Money □

Portable shovel □ Plates □ Knives and forks □ Clothing □

Camping Knife □ Rucksack □ Food Items □ Mobile Phone □

Mobile phone charger □ Solar charger □ Map □ Pen □

Water Purifying tablets □ First Aid Kit □ Binoculars □

Location of nearest Town/Village:

_____

Mode of transport? Foot □ Bike □ Motorbike □ Car □

Location of landowner/farm:_____

Permission obtained to camp here? Y □ N □

Date: ____/____/_____

Expected Duration of stay? 1 □ 2 □ 3 □ 4 □ 5 □ Nights

How was the stay?_____

Any problems? _____

Notes:

Camping Equipment Check List

Tent □ Fly-sheet □ Tent poles □ Ground sheet □ Bed roll □

Sleeping bag □ Pillow □ Tent pegs □ Rope □ Mallet □

Water container □ Lantern/torch □ Camping Gaz □

Matches □ Lighter □ Insect repellent □ Pans □ Money □

Portable shovel □ Plates □ Knives and forks □ Clothing □

Camping Knife □ Rucksack □ Food Items □ Mobile Phone □

Mobile phone charger □ Solar charger □ Map □ Pen □

Water Purifying tablets □ First Aid Kit □ Binoculars □

Location of nearest Town/Village:

_____

Mode of transport? Foot □ **Bike** □ **Motorbike** □ **Car** □

Location of landowner/farm:_____

Permission obtained to camp here? Y □ **N** □

Date: ____/____/_____

Expected Duration of stay? 1 □ **2** □ **3** □ **4** □ **5** □ **Nights**

How was the stay?_____

Any problems? _____

Notes:

Camping Equipment Check List

Tent □ Fly-sheet □ Tent poles □ Ground sheet □ Bed roll □

Sleeping bag □ Pillow □ Tent pegs □ Rope □ Mallet □

Water container □ Lantern/torch □ Camping Gaz □

Matches □ Lighter □ Insect repellent □ Pans □ Money □

Portable shovel □ Plates □ Knives and forks □ Clothing □

Camping Knife □ Rucksack □ Food Items □ Mobile Phone □

Mobile phone charger □ Solar charger □ Map □ Pen □

Water Purifying tablets □ First Aid Kit □ Binoculars □

Location of nearest Town/Village:

_____

Mode of transport? Foot □ Bike □ Motorbike □ Car □

Location of landowner/farm:_____

Permission obtained to camp here? Y □ N □

Date: ____/____/_____

Expected Duration of stay? 1 □ 2 □ 3 □ 4 □ 5 □ Nights

 How was the stay?_____

 Any problems? _____

Notes:

Camping Equipment Check List

Tent □ Fly-sheet □ Tent poles □ Ground sheet □ Bed roll □
Sleeping bag □ Pillow □ Tent pegs □ Rope □ Mallet □
Water container □ Lantern/torch □ Camping Gaz □
Matches □ Lighter □ Insect repellent □ Pans □ Money □
Portable shovel □ Plates □ Knives and forks □ Clothing □
Camping Knife □ Rucksack □ Food Items □ Mobile Phone □
Mobile phone charger □ Solar charger □ Map □ Pen □
Water Purifying tablets □ First Aid Kit □ Binoculars □

Location of nearest Town/Village:
_____

Mode of transport? Foot □ Bike □ Motorbike □ Car □
Location of landowner/farm:_____
Permission obtained to camp here? Y □ N □
Date: ____/____/_____
Expected Duration of stay? 1 □ 2 □ 3 □ 4 □ 5 □ Nights
 How was the stay?_____
 Any problems? _____
Notes:

Camping Equipment Check List

Tent □ Fly-sheet □ Tent poles □ Ground sheet □ Bed roll □
Sleeping bag □ Pillow □ Tent pegs □ Rope □ Mallet □
Water container □ Lantern/torch □ Camping Gaz □
Matches □ Lighter □ Insect repellent □ Pans □ Money □
Portable shovel □ Plates □ Knives and forks □ Clothing □
Camping Knife □ Rucksack □ Food Items □ Mobile Phone □
Mobile phone charger □ Solar charger □ Map □ Pen □
Water Purifying tablets □ First Aid Kit □ Binoculars □

Location of nearest Town/Village:

_____

Mode of transport? Foot □ Bike □ Motorbike □ Car □
Location of landowner/farm:_____
Permission obtained to camp here? Y □ N □
Date: ____/____/_____
Expected Duration of stay? 1 □ 2 □ 3 □ 4 □ 5 □ Nights
 How was the stay?_____
 Any problems? _____
Notes:

Camping Equipment Check List

Tent □ Fly-sheet □ Tent poles □ Ground sheet □ Bed roll □
Sleeping bag □ Pillow □ Tent pegs □ Rope □ Mallet □
Water container □ Lantern/torch □ Camping Gaz □
Matches □ Lighter □ Insect repellent □ Pans □ Money □
Portable shovel □ Plates □ Knives and forks □ Clothing □
Camping Knife □ Rucksack □ Food Items □ Mobile Phone □
Mobile phone charger □ Solar charger □ Map □ Pen □
Water Purifying tablets □ First Aid Kit □ Binoculars □

Location of nearest Town/Village:

_____

Mode of transport? Foot □ Bike □ Motorbike □ Car □

Location of landowner/farm:_____

Permission obtained to camp here? Y □ N □

Date: ____/____/_____

Expected Duration of stay? 1 □ 2 □ 3 □ 4 □ 5 □ Nights

How was the stay?_____

Any problems? _____

Notes:

Camping Equipment Check List

Tent □ Fly-sheet □ Tent poles □ Ground sheet □ Bed roll □
Sleeping bag □ Pillow □ Tent pegs □ Rope □ Mallet □
Water container □ Lantern/torch □ Camping Gaz □
Matches □ Lighter □ Insect repellent □ Pans □ Money □
Portable shovel □ Plates □ Knives and forks □ Clothing □
Camping Knife □ Rucksack □ Food Items □ Mobile Phone □
Mobile phone charger □ Solar charger □ Map □ Pen □
Water Purifying tablets □ First Aid Kit □ Binoculars □

Location of nearest Town/Village:

_____

Mode of transport? Foot □ Bike □ Motorbike □ Car □
Location of landowner/farm:_____
Permission obtained to camp here? Y □ N □
Date: _____/_____/_____
Expected Duration of stay? 1 □ 2 □ 3 □ 4 □ 5 □ Nights
How was the stay?_____
Any problems? _____
Notes:

Camping Equipment Check List

Tent □ Fly-sheet □ Tent poles □ Ground sheet □ Bed roll □

Sleeping bag □ Pillow □ Tent pegs □ Rope □ Mallet □

Water container □ Lantern/torch □ Camping Gaz □

Matches □ Lighter □ Insect repellent □ Pans □ Money □

Portable shovel □ Plates □ Knives and forks □ Clothing □

Camping Knife □ Rucksack □ Food Items □ Mobile Phone □

Mobile phone charger □ Solar charger □ Map □ Pen □

Water Purifying tablets □ First Aid Kit □ Binoculars □

Location of nearest Town/Village:

_____

Mode of transport? Foot □ Bike □ Motorbike □ Car □

Location of landowner/farm:_____

Permission obtained to camp here? Y □ N □

Date: ____/____/_____

Expected Duration of stay? 1 □ 2 □ 3 □ 4 □ 5 □ Nights

How was the stay?_____

Any problems? _____

Notes:

Camping Equipment Check List

Tent □ Fly-sheet □ Tent poles □ Ground sheet □ Bed roll □
Sleeping bag □ Pillow □ Tent pegs □ Rope □ Mallet □
Water container □ Lantern/torch □ Camping Gaz □
Matches □ Lighter □ Insect repellent □ Pans □ Money □
Portable shovel □ Plates □ Knives and forks □ Clothing □
Camping Knife □ Rucksack □ Food Items □ Mobile Phone □
Mobile phone charger □ Solar charger □ Map □ Pen □
Water Purifying tablets □ First Aid Kit □ Binoculars □

Location of nearest Town/Village:

_____

Mode of transport? Foot □ Bike □ Motorbike □ Car □
Location of landowner/farm:_____
Permission obtained to camp here? Y □ N □
Date: _____/_____/_____
Expected Duration of stay? 1 □ 2 □ 3 □ 4 □ 5 □ Nights
 How was the stay?_____
 Any problems? _____
Notes:

Camping Equipment Check List

Tent □ Fly-sheet □ Tent poles □ Ground sheet □ Bed roll □

Sleeping bag □ Pillow □ Tent pegs □ Rope □ Mallet □

Water container □ Lantern/torch □ Camping Gaz □

Matches □ Lighter □ Insect repellent □ Pans □ Money □

Portable shovel □ Plates □ Knives and forks □ Clothing □

Camping Knife □ Rucksack □ Food Items □ Mobile Phone □

Mobile phone charger □ Solar charger □ Map □ Pen □

Water Purifying tablets □ First Aid Kit □ Binoculars □

Location of nearest Town/Village:

_____

Mode of transport? Foot □ Bike □ Motorbike □ Car □

Location of landowner/farm:_____

Permission obtained to camp here? Y □ N □

Date: ____/____/_____

Expected Duration of stay? 1 □ 2 □ 3 □ 4 □ 5 □ Nights

 How was the stay?_____

 Any problems? _____

Notes:

Camping Equipment Check List

Tent □ Fly-sheet □ Tent poles □ Ground sheet □ Bed roll □

Sleeping bag □ Pillow □ Tent pegs □ Rope □ Mallet □

Water container □ Lantern/torch □ Camping Gaz □

Matches □ Lighter □ Insect repellent □ Pans □ Money □

Portable shovel □ Plates □ Knives and forks □ Clothing □

Camping Knife □ Rucksack □ Food Items □ Mobile Phone □

Mobile phone charger □ Solar charger □ Map □ Pen □

Water Purifying tablets □ First Aid Kit □ Binoculars □

Location of nearest Town/Village:

_____

Mode of transport? Foot □ Bike □ Motorbike □ Car □

Location of landowner/farm:_____

Permission obtained to camp here? Y □ N □

Date: ____/____/_____

Expected Duration of stay? 1 □ 2 □ 3 □ 4 □ 5 □ Nights

 How was the stay?_____

 Any problems? _____

Notes:

Camping Equipment Check List

Tent □ Fly-sheet □ Tent poles □ Ground sheet □ Bed roll □

Sleeping bag □ Pillow □ Tent pegs □ Rope □ Mallet □

Water container □ Lantern/torch □ Camping Gaz □

Matches □ Lighter □ Insect repellent □ Pans □ Money □

Portable shovel □ Plates □ Knives and forks □ Clothing □

Camping Knife □ Rucksack □ Food Items □ Mobile Phone □

Mobile phone charger □ Solar charger □ Map □ Pen □

Water Purifying tablets □ First Aid Kit □ Binoculars □

Location of nearest Town/Village:

_____

Mode of transport? Foot □ **Bike** □ **Motorbike** □ **Car** □

Location of landowner/farm:_____

Permission obtained to camp here? Y □ **N** □

Date: _____/_____/_____

Expected Duration of stay? 1 □ **2** □ **3** □ **4** □ **5** □ **Nights**

How was the stay?_____

Any problems? _____

Notes:

Camping Equipment Check List

Tent □ Fly-sheet □ Tent poles □ Ground sheet □ Bed roll □
Sleeping bag □ Pillow □ Tent pegs □ Rope □ Mallet □
Water container □ Lantern/torch □ Camping Gaz □
Matches □ Lighter □ Insect repellent □ Pans □ Money □
Portable shovel □ Plates □ Knives and forks □ Clothing □
Camping Knife □ Rucksack □ Food Items □ Mobile Phone □
Mobile phone charger □ Solar charger □ Map □ Pen □
Water Purifying tablets □ First Aid Kit □ Binoculars □

Location of nearest Town/Village:

_____

Mode of transport? Foot □ Bike □ Motorbike □ Car □
Location of landowner/farm:_____
Permission obtained to camp here? Y □ N □
Date: ____/____/_____
Expected Duration of stay? 1 □ 2 □ 3 □ 4 □ 5 □ Nights
 How was the stay?_____
 Any problems? _____
Notes:

Camping Equipment Check List

Tent □ Fly-sheet □ Tent poles □ Ground sheet □ Bed roll □

Sleeping bag □ Pillow □ Tent pegs □ Rope □ Mallet □

Water container □ Lantern/torch □ Camping Gaz □

Matches □ Lighter □ Insect repellent □ Pans □ Money □

Portable shovel □ Plates □ Knives and forks □ Clothing □

Camping Knife □ Rucksack □ Food Items □ Mobile Phone □

Mobile phone charger □ Solar charger □ Map □ Pen □

Water Purifying tablets □ First Aid Kit □ Binoculars □

Location of nearest Town/Village:

_____

Mode of transport? Foot □ Bike □ Motorbike □ Car □

Location of landowner/farm:_____

Permission obtained to camp here? Y □ N □

Date: ____/____/_____

Expected Duration of stay? 1 □ 2 □ 3 □ 4 □ 5 □ Nights

How was the stay?_____

Any problems? _____

Notes:

Camping Equipment Check List

Tent □ Fly-sheet □ Tent poles □ Ground sheet □ Bed roll □

Sleeping bag □ Pillow □ Tent pegs □ Rope □ Mallet □

Water container □ Lantern/torch □ Camping Gaz □

Matches □ Lighter □ Insect repellent □ Pans □ Money □

Portable shovel □ Plates □ Knives and forks □ Clothing □

Camping Knife □ Rucksack □ Food Items □ Mobile Phone □

Mobile phone charger □ Solar charger □ Map □ Pen □

Water Purifying tablets □ First Aid Kit □ Binoculars □

Location of nearest Town/Village:

_____

Mode of transport? Foot □ Bike □ Motorbike □ Car □

Location of landowner/farm:_____

Permission obtained to camp here? Y □ N □

Date: _____/_____/_____

Expected Duration of stay? 1 □ 2 □ 3 □ 4 □ 5 □ Nights

 How was the stay?_____

 Any problems? _____

Notes:

Camping Equipment Check List

Tent ☐ Fly-sheet ☐ Tent poles ☐ Ground sheet ☐ Bed roll ☐
Sleeping bag ☐ Pillow ☐ Tent pegs ☐ Rope ☐ Mallet ☐
Water container ☐ Lantern/torch ☐ Camping Gaz ☐
Matches ☐ Lighter ☐ Insect repellent ☐ Pans ☐ Money ☐
Portable shovel ☐ Plates ☐ Knives and forks ☐ Clothing ☐
Camping Knife ☐ Rucksack ☐ Food Items ☐ Mobile Phone ☐
Mobile phone charger ☐ Solar charger ☐ Map ☐ Pen ☐
Water Purifying tablets ☐ First Aid Kit ☐ Binoculars ☐

Location of nearest Town/Village:
_____

Mode of transport? Foot ☐ Bike ☐ Motorbike ☐ Car ☐
Location of landowner/farm:_____
Permission obtained to camp here? Y ☐ N ☐
Date: ____/____/_____
Expected Duration of stay? 1 ☐ 2 ☐ 3 ☐ 4 ☐ 5 ☐ Nights
 How was the stay?_____
 Any problems? _____
Notes:

Camping Equipment Check List

Tent □ Fly-sheet □ Tent poles □ Ground sheet □ Bed roll □
Sleeping bag □ Pillow □ Tent pegs □ Rope □ Mallet □
Water container □ Lantern/torch □ Camping Gaz □
Matches □ Lighter □ Insect repellent □ Pans □ Money □
Portable shovel □ Plates □ Knives and forks □ Clothing □
Camping Knife □ Rucksack □ Food Items □ Mobile Phone □
Mobile phone charger □ Solar charger □ Map □ Pen □
Water Purifying tablets □ First Aid Kit □ Binoculars □

Location of nearest Town/Village:

_____

Mode of transport? Foot □ Bike □ Motorbike □ Car □
Location of landowner/farm:_____
Permission obtained to camp here? Y □ N □
Date: ____/____/_____
Expected Duration of stay? 1 □ 2 □ 3 □ 4 □ 5 □ Nights
 How was the stay?_____
 Any problems? _____
Notes:

Camping Equipment Check List

Tent □ Fly-sheet □ Tent poles □ Ground sheet □ Bed roll □
Sleeping bag □ Pillow □ Tent pegs □ Rope □ Mallet □
Water container □ Lantern/torch □ Camping Gaz □
Matches □ Lighter □ Insect repellent □ Pans □ Money □
Portable shovel □ Plates □ Knives and forks □ Clothing □
Camping Knife □ Rucksack □ Food Items □ Mobile Phone □
Mobile phone charger □ Solar charger □ Map □ Pen □
Water Purifying tablets □ First Aid Kit □ Binoculars □

Location of nearest Town/Village:
_____

Mode of transport? Foot □ **Bike** □ **Motorbike** □ **Car** □
Location of landowner/farm:_____

Permission obtained to camp here? Y □ **N** □

Date: _____/_____/_____

Expected Duration of stay? 1 □ **2** □ **3** □ **4** □ **5** □ **Nights**

 How was the stay?_____

 Any problems? _____

Notes:

Camping Equipment Check List

Tent □ Fly-sheet □ Tent poles □ Ground sheet □ Bed roll □
Sleeping bag □ Pillow □ Tent pegs □ Rope □ Mallet □
Water container □ Lantern/torch □ Camping Gaz □
Matches □ Lighter □ Insect repellent □ Pans □ Money □
Portable shovel □ Plates □ Knives and forks □ Clothing □
Camping Knife □ Rucksack □ Food Items □ Mobile Phone □
Mobile phone charger □ Solar charger □ Map □ Pen □
Water Purifying tablets □ First Aid Kit □ Binoculars □

Location of nearest Town/Village:

_____

Mode of transport? Foot □ Bike □ Motorbike □ Car □
Location of landowner/farm:_____
Permission obtained to camp here? Y □ N □
Date: ____/____/_____
Expected Duration of stay? 1 □ 2 □ 3 □ 4 □ 5 □ Nights
 How was the stay?_____
 Any problems? _____
Notes:

Camping Equipment Check List

Tent □ Fly-sheet □ Tent poles □ Ground sheet □ Bed roll □

Sleeping bag □ Pillow □ Tent pegs □ Rope □ Mallet □

Water container □ Lantern/torch □ Camping Gaz □

Matches □ Lighter □ Insect repellent □ Pans □ Money □

Portable shovel □ Plates □ Knives and forks □ Clothing □

Camping Knife □ Rucksack □ Food Items □ Mobile Phone □

Mobile phone charger □ Solar charger □ Map □ Pen □

Water Purifying tablets □ First Aid Kit □ Binoculars □

Location of nearest Town/Village:

_____

Mode of transport? Foot □ Bike □ Motorbike □ Car □

Location of landowner/farm:_____

Permission obtained to camp here? Y □ N □

Date: ____/____/_____

Expected Duration of stay? 1 □ 2 □ 3 □ 4 □ 5 □ Nights

 How was the stay?_____

 Any problems? _____

Notes:

Camping Equipment Check List

Tent □ Fly-sheet □ Tent poles □ Ground sheet □ Bed roll □
Sleeping bag □ Pillow □ Tent pegs □ Rope □ Mallet □
Water container □ Lantern/torch □ Camping Gaz □
Matches □ Lighter □ Insect repellent □ Pans □ Money □
Portable shovel □ Plates □ Knives and forks □ Clothing □
Camping Knife □ Rucksack □ Food Items □ Mobile Phone □
Mobile phone charger □ Solar charger □ Map □ Pen □
Water Purifying tablets □ First Aid Kit □ Binoculars □

Location of nearest Town/Village:

_____

Mode of transport? Foot □ Bike □ Motorbike □ Car □
Location of landowner/farm:_____
Permission obtained to camp here? Y □ N □
Date: ____/____/_____
Expected Duration of stay? 1 □ 2 □ 3 □ 4 □ 5 □ Nights
How was the stay?_____
Any problems? _____
Notes:

Camping Equipment Check List

Tent □ Fly-sheet □ Tent poles □ Ground sheet □ Bed roll □

Sleeping bag □ Pillow □ Tent pegs □ Rope □ Mallet □

Water container □ Lantern/torch □ Camping Gaz □

Matches □ Lighter □ Insect repellent □ Pans □ Money □

Portable shovel □ Plates □ Knives and forks □ Clothing □

Camping Knife □ Rucksack □ Food Items □ Mobile Phone □

Mobile phone charger □ Solar charger □ Map □ Pen □

Water Purifying tablets □ First Aid Kit □ Binoculars □

Location of nearest Town/Village:

_____

Mode of transport? Foot □ Bike □ Motorbike □ Car □

Location of landowner/farm:_____

Permission obtained to camp here? Y □ N □

Date: ____/____/_____

Expected Duration of stay? 1 □ 2 □ 3 □ 4 □ 5 □ Nights

How was the stay?_____

Any problems? _____

Notes:

Camping Equipment Check List

Tent □ Fly-sheet □ Tent poles □ Ground sheet □ Bed roll □
Sleeping bag □ Pillow □ Tent pegs □ Rope □ Mallet □
Water container □ Lantern/torch □ Camping Gaz □
Matches □ Lighter □ Insect repellent □ Pans □ Money □
Portable shovel □ Plates □ Knives and forks □ Clothing □
Camping Knife □ Rucksack □ Food Items □ Mobile Phone □
Mobile phone charger □ Solar charger □ Map □ Pen □
Water Purifying tablets □ First Aid Kit □ Binoculars □

Location of nearest Town/Village:
_____

Mode of transport? Foot □ Bike □ Motorbike □ Car □
Location of landowner/farm:_____
Permission obtained to camp here? Y □ N □
Date: _____/_____/_____
Expected Duration of stay? 1 □ 2 □ 3 □ 4 □ 5 □ Nights
How was the stay?_____
Any problems? _____
Notes:

Camping Equipment Check List

Tent □ Fly-sheet □ Tent poles □ Ground sheet □ Bed roll □

Sleeping bag □ Pillow □ Tent pegs □ Rope □ Mallet □

Water container □ Lantern/torch □ Camping Gaz □

Matches □ Lighter □ Insect repellent □ Pans □ Money □

Portable shovel □ Plates □ Knives and forks □ Clothing □

Camping Knife □ Rucksack □ Food Items □ Mobile Phone □

Mobile phone charger □ Solar charger □ Map □ Pen □

Water Purifying tablets □ First Aid Kit □ Binoculars □

Location of nearest Town/Village:

_____

Mode of transport? Foot □ Bike □ Motorbike □ Car □

Location of landowner/farm:_____

Permission obtained to camp here? Y □ N □

Date: ____/____/_____

Expected Duration of stay? 1 □ 2 □ 3 □ 4 □ 5 □ Nights

How was the stay?_____

Any problems? _____

Notes:

Camping Equipment Check List

Tent □ Fly-sheet □ Tent poles □ Ground sheet □ Bed roll □

Sleeping bag □ Pillow □ Tent pegs □ Rope □ Mallet □

Water container □ Lantern/torch □ Camping Gaz □

Matches □ Lighter □ Insect repellent □ Pans □ Money □

Portable shovel □ Plates □ Knives and forks □ Clothing □

Camping Knife □ Rucksack □ Food Items □ Mobile Phone □

Mobile phone charger □ Solar charger □ Map □ Pen □

Water Purifying tablets □ First Aid Kit □ Binoculars □

Location of nearest Town/Village:

_____

Mode of transport? Foot □ Bike □ Motorbike □ Car □

Location of landowner/farm:_____

Permission obtained to camp here? Y □ N □

Date: _____/_____/_____

Expected Duration of stay? 1 □ 2 □ 3 □ 4 □ 5 □ Nights

How was the stay?_____

Any problems? _____

Notes:

Camping Equipment Check List

Tent □ Fly-sheet □ Tent poles □ Ground sheet □ Bed roll □

Sleeping bag □ Pillow □ Tent pegs □ Rope □ Mallet □

Water container □ Lantern/torch □ Camping Gaz □

Matches □ Lighter □ Insect repellent □ Pans □ Money □

Portable shovel □ Plates □ Knives and forks □ Clothing □

Camping Knife □ Rucksack □ Food Items □ Mobile Phone □

Mobile phone charger □ Solar charger □ Map □ Pen □

Water Purifying tablets □ First Aid Kit □ Binoculars □

Location of nearest Town/Village:

_____

Mode of transport? Foot □ Bike □ Motorbike □ Car □

Location of landowner/farm:_____

Permission obtained to camp here? Y □ N □

Date: ____/____/_____

Expected Duration of stay? 1 □ 2 □ 3 □ 4 □ 5 □ Nights

How was the stay?_____

Any problems? _____

Notes:

Camping Equipment Check List

Tent □ Fly-sheet □ Tent poles □ Ground sheet □ Bed roll □
Sleeping bag □ Pillow □ Tent pegs □ Rope □ Mallet □
Water container □ Lantern/torch □ Camping Gaz □
Matches □ Lighter □ Insect repellent □ Pans □ Money □
Portable shovel □ Plates □ Knives and forks □ Clothing □
Camping Knife □ Rucksack □ Food Items □ Mobile Phone □
Mobile phone charger □ Solar charger □ Map □ Pen □
Water Purifying tablets □ First Aid Kit □ Binoculars □

Location of nearest Town/Village:

_____

Mode of transport? Foot □ Bike □ Motorbike □ Car □
Location of landowner/farm:_____
Permission obtained to camp here? Y □ N □
Date: ____/____/_____
Expected Duration of stay? 1 □ 2 □ 3 □ 4 □ 5 □ Nights
 How was the stay?_____
 Any problems? _____
Notes:

Camping Equipment Check List

Tent □ Fly-sheet □ Tent poles □ Ground sheet □ Bed roll □
Sleeping bag □ Pillow □ Tent pegs □ Rope □ Mallet □
Water container □ Lantern/torch □ Camping Gaz □
Matches □ Lighter □ Insect repellent □ Pans □ Money □
Portable shovel □ Plates □ Knives and forks □ Clothing □
Camping Knife □ Rucksack □ Food Items □ Mobile Phone □
Mobile phone charger □ Solar charger □ Map □ Pen □
Water Purifying tablets □ First Aid Kit □ Binoculars □

Location of nearest Town/Village:

_____

Mode of transport? Foot □ Bike □ Motorbike □ Car □

Location of landowner/farm:_____

Permission obtained to camp here? Y □ N □

Date: ____/____/_____

Expected Duration of stay? 1 □ 2 □ 3 □ 4 □ 5 □ Nights

How was the stay?_____

Any problems? _____

Notes:

Camping Equipment Check List

Tent □ Fly-sheet □ Tent poles □ Ground sheet □ Bed roll □
Sleeping bag □ Pillow □ Tent pegs □ Rope □ Mallet □
Water container □ Lantern/torch □ Camping Gaz □
Matches □ Lighter □ Insect repellent □ Pans □ Money □
Portable shovel □ Plates □ Knives and forks □ Clothing □
Camping Knife □ Rucksack □ Food Items □ Mobile Phone □
Mobile phone charger □ Solar charger □ Map □ Pen □
Water Purifying tablets □ First Aid Kit □ Binoculars □

Location of nearest Town/Village:

_____

Mode of transport? Foot □ Bike □ Motorbike □ Car □
Location of landowner/farm:_____
Permission obtained to camp here? Y □ N □
Date: ____/____/_____
Expected Duration of stay? 1 □ 2 □ 3 □ 4 □ 5 □ Nights
 How was the stay?_____
 Any problems? _____
Notes:

Camping Equipment Check List

Tent □ Fly-sheet □ Tent poles □ Ground sheet □ Bed roll □
Sleeping bag □ Pillow □ Tent pegs □ Rope □ Mallet □
Water container □ Lantern/torch □ Camping Gaz □
Matches □ Lighter □ Insect repellent □ Pans □ Money □
Portable shovel □ Plates □ Knives and forks □ Clothing □
Camping Knife □ Rucksack □ Food Items □ Mobile Phone □
Mobile phone charger □ Solar charger □ Map □ Pen □
Water Purifying tablets □ First Aid Kit □ Binoculars □

Location of nearest Town/Village:
_____

Mode of transport? Foot □ Bike □ Motorbike □ Car □

Location of landowner/farm:_____

Permission obtained to camp here? Y □ N □

Date: ____/____/_____

Expected Duration of stay? 1 □ 2 □ 3 □ 4 □ 5 □ Nights

How was the stay?_____

Any problems? _____

Notes:

Camping Equipment Check List

Tent □ Fly-sheet □ Tent poles □ Ground sheet □ Bed roll □
Sleeping bag □ Pillow □ Tent pegs □ Rope □ Mallet □
Water container □ Lantern/torch □ Camping Gaz □
Matches □ Lighter □ Insect repellent □ Pans □ Money □
Portable shovel □ Plates □ Knives and forks □ Clothing □
Camping Knife □ Rucksack □ Food Items □ Mobile Phone □
Mobile phone charger □ Solar charger □ Map □ Pen □
Water Purifying tablets □ First Aid Kit □ Binoculars □

Location of nearest Town/Village:

_____

Mode of transport? Foot □ Bike □ Motorbike □ Car □

Location of landowner/farm:_____

Permission obtained to camp here? Y □ N □

Date: ____/____/_____

Expected Duration of stay? 1 □ 2 □ 3 □ 4 □ 5 □ Nights

How was the stay?_____

Any problems? _____

Notes:

Camping Equipment Check List

Tent □ Fly-sheet □ Tent poles □ Ground sheet □ Bed roll □
Sleeping bag □ Pillow □ Tent pegs □ Rope □ Mallet □
Water container □ Lantern/torch □ Camping Gaz □
Matches □ Lighter □ Insect repellent □ Pans □ Money □
Portable shovel □ Plates □ Knives and forks □ Clothing □
Camping Knife □ Rucksack □ Food Items □ Mobile Phone □
Mobile phone charger □ Solar charger □ Map □ Pen □
Water Purifying tablets □ First Aid Kit □ Binoculars □

Location of nearest Town/Village:

_____

Mode of transport? Foot □ Bike □ Motorbike □ Car □

Location of landowner/farm:_____

Permission obtained to camp here? Y □ N □

Date: ____/____/_____

Expected Duration of stay? 1 □ 2 □ 3 □ 4 □ 5 □ Nights

How was the stay?_____

Any problems? _____

Notes:

Camping Equipment Check List

Tent □ Fly-sheet □ Tent poles □ Ground sheet □ Bed roll □

Sleeping bag □ Pillow □ Tent pegs □ Rope □ Mallet □

Water container □ Lantern/torch □ Camping Gaz □

Matches □ Lighter □ Insect repellent □ Pans □ Money □

Portable shovel □ Plates □ Knives and forks □ Clothing □

Camping Knife □ Rucksack □ Food Items □ Mobile Phone □

Mobile phone charger □ Solar charger □ Map □ Pen □

Water Purifying tablets □ First Aid Kit □ Binoculars □

Location of nearest Town/Village:

_____

Mode of transport? Foot □ Bike □ Motorbike □ Car □

Location of landowner/farm:_____

Permission obtained to camp here? Y □ N □

Date: _____/_____/_____

Expected Duration of stay? 1 □ 2 □ 3 □ 4 □ 5 □ Nights

How was the stay?_____

Any problems? _____

Notes:

Camping Equipment Check List

Tent ☐ Fly-sheet ☐ Tent poles ☐ Ground sheet ☐ Bed roll ☐
Sleeping bag ☐ Pillow ☐ Tent pegs ☐ Rope ☐ Mallet ☐
Water container ☐ Lantern/torch ☐ Camping Gaz ☐
Matches ☐ Lighter ☐ Insect repellent ☐ Pans ☐ Money ☐
Portable shovel ☐ Plates ☐ Knives and forks ☐ Clothing ☐
Camping Knife ☐ Rucksack ☐ Food Items ☐ Mobile Phone ☐
Mobile phone charger ☐ Solar charger ☐ Map ☐ Pen ☐
Water Purifying tablets ☐ First Aid Kit ☐ Binoculars ☐

Location of nearest Town/Village:

_____

Mode of transport? Foot ☐ Bike ☐ Motorbike ☐ Car ☐
Location of landowner/farm:_____
Permission obtained to camp here? Y ☐ N ☐
Date: ____/____/_____
Expected Duration of stay? 1 ☐ 2 ☐ 3 ☐ 4 ☐ 5 ☐ Nights
 How was the stay?_____
 Any problems? _____
Notes:

Camping Equipment Check List

Tent □ Fly-sheet □ Tent poles □ Ground sheet □ Bed roll □

Sleeping bag □ Pillow □ Tent pegs □ Rope □ Mallet □

Water container □ Lantern/torch □ Camping Gaz □

Matches □ Lighter □ Insect repellent □ Pans □ Money □

Portable shovel □ Plates □ Knives and forks □ Clothing □

Camping Knife □ Rucksack □ Food Items □ Mobile Phone □

Mobile phone charger □ Solar charger □ Map □ Pen □

Water Purifying tablets □ First Aid Kit □ Binoculars □

Location of nearest Town/Village:

_____

Mode of transport? Foot □ Bike □ Motorbike □ Car □

Location of landowner/farm:_____

Permission obtained to camp here? Y □ N □

Date: ____/____/_____

Expected Duration of stay? 1 □ 2 □ 3 □ 4 □ 5 □ Nights

 How was the stay?_____

 Any problems? _____

Notes:

Camping Equipment Check List

Tent □ Fly-sheet □ Tent poles □ Ground sheet □ Bed roll □
Sleeping bag □ Pillow □ Tent pegs □ Rope □ Mallet □
Water container □ Lantern/torch □ Camping Gaz □
Matches □ Lighter □ Insect repellent □ Pans □ Money □
Portable shovel □ Plates □ Knives and forks □ Clothing □
Camping Knife □ Rucksack □ Food Items □ Mobile Phone □
Mobile phone charger □ Solar charger □ Map □ Pen □
Water Purifying tablets □ First Aid Kit □ Binoculars □

Location of nearest Town/Village:

_____

Mode of transport? Foot □ Bike □ Motorbike □ Car □
Location of landowner/farm:_____
Permission obtained to camp here? Y □ N □
Date: ____/____/_____
Expected Duration of stay? 1 □ 2 □ 3 □ 4 □ 5 □ Nights
 How was the stay?_____
 Any problems? _____
Notes:

Camping Equipment Check List

Tent □ Fly-sheet □ Tent poles □ Ground sheet □ Bed roll □

Sleeping bag □ Pillow □ Tent pegs □ Rope □ Mallet □

Water container □ Lantern/torch □ Camping Gaz □

Matches □ Lighter □ Insect repellent □ Pans □ Money □

Portable shovel □ Plates □ Knives and forks □ Clothing □

Camping Knife □ Rucksack □ Food Items □ Mobile Phone □

Mobile phone charger □ Solar charger □ Map □ Pen □

Water Purifying tablets □ First Aid Kit □ Binoculars □

Location of nearest Town/Village:

_____

Mode of transport? Foot □ Bike □ Motorbike □ Car □

Location of landowner/farm:_____

Permission obtained to camp here? Y □ N □

Date: ____/____/_____

Expected Duration of stay? 1 □ 2 □ 3 □ 4 □ 5 □ Nights

How was the stay?_____

Any problems? _____

Notes:

Camping Equipment Check List

Tent □ Fly-sheet □ Tent poles □ Ground sheet □ Bed roll □
Sleeping bag □ Pillow □ Tent pegs □ Rope □ Mallet □
Water container □ Lantern/torch □ Camping Gaz □
Matches □ Lighter □ Insect repellent □ Pans □ Money □
Portable shovel □ Plates □ Knives and forks □ Clothing □
Camping Knife □ Rucksack □ Food Items □ Mobile Phone □
Mobile phone charger □ Solar charger □ Map □ Pen □
Water Purifying tablets □ First Aid Kit □ Binoculars □

Location of nearest Town/Village:
_____

Mode of transport? Foot □ Bike □ Motorbike □ Car □

Location of landowner/farm:_____

Permission obtained to camp here? Y □ N □

Date: ____/____/_____

Expected Duration of stay? 1 □ 2 □ 3 □ 4 □ 5 □ Nights

 How was the stay?_____

 Any problems? _____

Notes:

Camping Equipment Check List

Tent □ Fly-sheet □ Tent poles □ Ground sheet □ Bed roll □

Sleeping bag □ Pillow □ Tent pegs □ Rope □ Mallet □

Water container □ Lantern/torch □ Camping Gaz □

Matches □ Lighter □ Insect repellent □ Pans □ Money □

Portable shovel □ Plates □ Knives and forks □ Clothing □

Camping Knife □ Rucksack □ Food Items □ Mobile Phone □

Mobile phone charger □ Solar charger □ Map □ Pen □

Water Purifying tablets □ First Aid Kit □ Binoculars □

Location of nearest Town/Village:

_____

Mode of transport? Foot □ Bike □ Motorbike □ Car □

Location of landowner/farm:_____

Permission obtained to camp here? Y □ N □

Date: ____/____/_____

Expected Duration of stay? 1 □ 2 □ 3 □ 4 □ 5 □ Nights

 How was the stay?_____

 Any problems? _____

Notes:

Camping Equipment Check List

Tent □ Fly-sheet □ Tent poles □ Ground sheet □ Bed roll □

Sleeping bag □ Pillow □ Tent pegs □ Rope □ Mallet □

Water container □ Lantern/torch □ Camping Gaz □

Matches □ Lighter □ Insect repellent □ Pans □ Money □

Portable shovel □ Plates □ Knives and forks □ Clothing □

Camping Knife □ Rucksack □ Food Items □ Mobile Phone □

Mobile phone charger □ Solar charger □ Map □ Pen □

Water Purifying tablets □ First Aid Kit □ Binoculars □

Location of nearest Town/Village:

_____

Mode of transport? Foot □ Bike □ Motorbike □ Car □

Location of landowner/farm:_____

Permission obtained to camp here? Y □ N □

Date: ____/____/_____

Expected Duration of stay? 1 □ 2 □ 3 □ 4 □ 5 □ Nights

How was the stay?_____

Any problems? _____

Notes:

Camping Equipment Check List

Tent □ Fly-sheet □ Tent poles □ Ground sheet □ Bed roll □

Sleeping bag □ Pillow □ Tent pegs □ Rope □ Mallet □

Water container □ Lantern/torch □ Camping Gaz □

Matches □ Lighter □ Insect repellent □ Pans □ Money □

Portable shovel □ Plates □ Knives and forks □ Clothing □

Camping Knife □ Rucksack □ Food Items □ Mobile Phone □

Mobile phone charger □ Solar charger □ Map □ Pen □

Water Purifying tablets □ First Aid Kit □ Binoculars □

Location of nearest Town/Village:

_____

Mode of transport? Foot □ Bike □ Motorbike □ Car □

Location of landowner/farm:_____

Permission obtained to camp here? Y □ N □

Date: _____/_____/_____

Expected Duration of stay? 1 □ 2 □ 3 □ 4 □ 5 □ Nights

 How was the stay?_____

 Any problems? _____

Notes:

Camping Equipment Check List

Tent □ Fly-sheet □ Tent poles □ Ground sheet □ Bed roll □

Sleeping bag □ Pillow □ Tent pegs □ Rope □ Mallet □

Water container □ Lantern/torch □ Camping Gaz □

Matches □ Lighter □ Insect repellent □ Pans □ Money □

Portable shovel □ Plates □ Knives and forks □ Clothing □

Camping Knife □ Rucksack □ Food Items □ Mobile Phone □

Mobile phone charger □ Solar charger □ Map □ Pen □

Water Purifying tablets □ First Aid Kit □ Binoculars □

Location of nearest Town/Village:

_____

Mode of transport? Foot □ Bike □ Motorbike □ Car □

Location of landowner/farm:_____

Permission obtained to camp here? Y □ N □

Date: _____/_____/_____

Expected Duration of stay? 1 □ 2 □ 3 □ 4 □ 5 □ Nights

How was the stay?_____

Any problems? _____

Notes:

Camping Equipment Check List

Tent □ Fly-sheet □ Tent poles □ Ground sheet □ Bed roll □

Sleeping bag □ Pillow □ Tent pegs □ Rope □ Mallet □

Water container □ Lantern/torch □ Camping Gaz □

Matches □ Lighter □ Insect repellent □ Pans □ Money □

Portable shovel □ Plates □ Knives and forks □ Clothing □

Camping Knife □ Rucksack □ Food Items □ Mobile Phone □

Mobile phone charger □ Solar charger □ Map □ Pen □

Water Purifying tablets □ First Aid Kit □ Binoculars □

Location of nearest Town/Village:

_____

Mode of transport? Foot □ Bike □ Motorbike □ Car □

Location of landowner/farm:_____

Permission obtained to camp here? Y □ N □

Date: ____/____/_____

Expected Duration of stay? 1 □ 2 □ 3 □ 4 □ 5 □ Nights

 How was the stay?_____

 Any problems? _____

Notes:

Camping Equipment Check List

Tent □ Fly-sheet □ Tent poles □ Ground sheet □ Bed roll □

Sleeping bag □ Pillow □ Tent pegs □ Rope □ Mallet □

Water container □ Lantern/torch □ Camping Gaz □

Matches □ Lighter □ Insect repellent □ Pans □ Money □

Portable shovel □ Plates □ Knives and forks □ Clothing □

Camping Knife □ Rucksack □ Food Items □ Mobile Phone □

Mobile phone charger □ Solar charger □ Map □ Pen □

Water Purifying tablets □ First Aid Kit □ Binoculars □

Location of nearest Town/Village:

_____

Mode of transport? Foot □ Bike □ Motorbike □ Car □

Location of landowner/farm:_____

Permission obtained to camp here? Y □ N □

Date: _____/_____/_____

Expected Duration of stay? 1 □ 2 □ 3 □ 4 □ 5 □ Nights

How was the stay?_____

Any problems? _____

Notes:

Camping Equipment Check List

Tent □ Fly-sheet □ Tent poles □ Ground sheet □ Bed roll □
Sleeping bag □ Pillow □ Tent pegs □ Rope □ Mallet □
Water container □ Lantern/torch □ Camping Gaz □
Matches □ Lighter □ Insect repellent □ Pans □ Money □
Portable shovel □ Plates □ Knives and forks □ Clothing □
Camping Knife □ Rucksack □ Food Items □ Mobile Phone □
Mobile phone charger □ Solar charger □ Map □ Pen □
Water Purifying tablets □ First Aid Kit □ Binoculars □

Location of nearest Town/Village:

_____

Mode of transport? Foot □ Bike □ Motorbike □ Car □
Location of landowner/farm:_____
Permission obtained to camp here? Y □ N □
Date: _____/_____/_____
Expected Duration of stay? 1 □ 2 □ 3 □ 4 □ 5 □ Nights
 How was the stay?_____
 Any problems? _____
Notes:

Camping Equipment Check List

Tent □ Fly-sheet □ Tent poles □ Ground sheet □ Bed roll □

Sleeping bag □ Pillow □ Tent pegs □ Rope □ Mallet □

Water container □ Lantern/torch □ Camping Gaz □

Matches □ Lighter □ Insect repellent □ Pans □ Money □

Portable shovel □ Plates □ Knives and forks □ Clothing □

Camping Knife □ Rucksack □ Food Items □ Mobile Phone □

Mobile phone charger □ Solar charger □ Map □ Pen □

Water Purifying tablets □ First Aid Kit □ Binoculars □

Location of nearest Town/Village:

_____

Mode of transport? Foot □ Bike □ Motorbike □ Car □

Location of landowner/farm:_____

Permission obtained to camp here? Y □ N □

Date: ____/____/_____

Expected Duration of stay? 1 □ 2 □ 3 □ 4 □ 5 □ Nights

How was the stay?_____

Any problems? _____

Notes:

Camping Equipment Check List

Tent □ Fly-sheet □ Tent poles □ Ground sheet □ Bed roll □
Sleeping bag □ Pillow □ Tent pegs □ Rope □ Mallet □
Water container □ Lantern/torch □ Camping Gaz □
Matches □ Lighter □ Insect repellent □ Pans □ Money □
Portable shovel □ Plates □ Knives and forks □ Clothing □
Camping Knife □ Rucksack □ Food Items □ Mobile Phone □
Mobile phone charger □ Solar charger □ Map □ Pen □
Water Purifying tablets □ First Aid Kit □ Binoculars □

Location of nearest Town/Village:

_____

Mode of transport? Foot □ Bike □ Motorbike □ Car □

Location of landowner/farm:_____

Permission obtained to camp here? Y □ N □

Date: ____/____/_____

Expected Duration of stay? 1 □ 2 □ 3 □ 4 □ 5 □ Nights

 How was the stay?_____

 Any problems? _____

Notes:

Camping Equipment Check List

Tent □ Fly-sheet □ Tent poles □ Ground sheet □ Bed roll □

Sleeping bag □ Pillow □ Tent pegs □ Rope □ Mallet □

Water container □ Lantern/torch □ Camping Gaz □

Matches □ Lighter □ Insect repellent □ Pans □ Money □

Portable shovel □ Plates □ Knives and forks □ Clothing □

Camping Knife □ Rucksack □ Food Items □ Mobile Phone □

Mobile phone charger □ Solar charger □ Map □ Pen □

Water Purifying tablets □ First Aid Kit □ Binoculars □

Location of nearest Town/Village:
_____

Mode of transport? Foot □ Bike □ Motorbike □ Car □

Location of landowner/farm:_____

Permission obtained to camp here? Y □ N □

Date: ____/____/_____

Expected Duration of stay? 1 □ 2 □ 3 □ 4 □ 5 □ Nights

 How was the stay?_____

 Any problems? _____

Notes:

Camping Equipment Check List

Tent □ Fly-sheet □ Tent poles □ Ground sheet □ Bed roll □
Sleeping bag □ Pillow □ Tent pegs □ Rope □ Mallet □
Water container □ Lantern/torch □ Camping Gaz □
Matches □ Lighter □ Insect repellent □ Pans □ Money □
Portable shovel □ Plates □ Knives and forks □ Clothing □
Camping Knife □ Rucksack □ Food Items □ Mobile Phone □
Mobile phone charger □ Solar charger □ Map □ Pen □
Water Purifying tablets □ First Aid Kit □ Binoculars □

Location of nearest Town/Village:

_____

Mode of transport? Foot □ Bike □ Motorbike □ Car □
Location of landowner/farm:_____
Permission obtained to camp here? Y □ N □
Date: _____/_____/_____
Expected Duration of stay? 1 □ 2 □ 3 □ 4 □ 5 □ Nights
 How was the stay?_____
 Any problems? _____
Notes:

Camping Equipment Check List

Tent □ Fly-sheet □ Tent poles □ Ground sheet □ Bed roll □
Sleeping bag □ Pillow □ Tent pegs □ Rope □ Mallet □
Water container □ Lantern/torch □ Camping Gaz □
Matches □ Lighter □ Insect repellent □ Pans □ Money □
Portable shovel □ Plates □ Knives and forks □ Clothing □
Camping Knife □ Rucksack □ Food Items □ Mobile Phone □
Mobile phone charger □ Solar charger □ Map □ Pen □
Water Purifying tablets □ First Aid Kit □ Binoculars □

Location of nearest Town/Village:

_____

Mode of transport? Foot □ Bike □ Motorbike □ Car □
Location of landowner/farm:_____
Permission obtained to camp here? Y □ N □
Date: ____/____/_____
Expected Duration of stay? 1 □ 2 □ 3 □ 4 □ 5 □ Nights
 How was the stay?_____
 Any problems? _____
Notes:

Camping Equipment Check List

Tent □ Fly-sheet □ Tent poles □ Ground sheet □ Bed roll □
Sleeping bag □ Pillow □ Tent pegs □ Rope □ Mallet □
Water container □ Lantern/torch □ Camping Gaz □
Matches □ Lighter □ Insect repellent □ Pans □ Money □
Portable shovel □ Plates □ Knives and forks □ Clothing □
Camping Knife □ Rucksack □ Food Items □ Mobile Phone □
Mobile phone charger □ Solar charger □ Map □ Pen □
Water Purifying tablets □ First Aid Kit □ Binoculars □

Location of nearest Town/Village:

_____

Mode of transport? Foot □ Bike □ Motorbike □ Car □
Location of landowner/farm:_____
Permission obtained to camp here? Y □ N □
Date: ____/____/_____
Expected Duration of stay? 1 □ 2 □ 3 □ 4 □ 5 □ Nights
 How was the stay?_____
 Any problems? _____
Notes:

Camping Equipment Check List

Tent □ Fly-sheet □ Tent poles □ Ground sheet □ Bed roll □

Sleeping bag □ Pillow □ Tent pegs □ Rope □ Mallet □

Water container □ Lantern/torch □ Camping Gaz □

Matches □ Lighter □ Insect repellent □ Pans □ Money □

Portable shovel □ Plates □ Knives and forks □ Clothing □

Camping Knife □ Rucksack □ Food Items □ Mobile Phone □

Mobile phone charger □ Solar charger □ Map □ Pen □

Water Purifying tablets □ First Aid Kit □ Binoculars □

Location of nearest Town/Village:

_____

Mode of transport? Foot □ Bike □ Motorbike □ Car □

Location of landowner/farm:_____

Permission obtained to camp here? Y □ N □

Date: _____/_____/_____

Expected Duration of stay? 1 □ 2 □ 3 □ 4 □ 5 □ Nights

How was the stay?_____

Any problems? _____

Notes:

Camping Equipment Check List

Tent □ Fly-sheet □ Tent poles □ Ground sheet □ Bed roll □
Sleeping bag □ Pillow □ Tent pegs □ Rope □ Mallet □
Water container □ Lantern/torch □ Camping Gaz □
Matches □ Lighter □ Insect repellent □ Pans □ Money □
Portable shovel □ Plates □ Knives and forks □ Clothing □
Camping Knife □ Rucksack □ Food Items □ Mobile Phone □
Mobile phone charger □ Solar charger □ Map □ Pen □
Water Purifying tablets □ First Aid Kit □ Binoculars □

Location of nearest Town/Village:

_____

Mode of transport? Foot □ Bike □ Motorbike □ Car □

Location of landowner/farm:_____

Permission obtained to camp here? Y □ N □

Date: ____/____/_____

Expected Duration of stay? 1 □ 2 □ 3 □ 4 □ 5 □ Nights

How was the stay?_____

Any problems? _____

Notes:

Camping Equipment Check List

Tent □ Fly-sheet □ Tent poles □ Ground sheet □ Bed roll □

Sleeping bag □ Pillow □ Tent pegs □ Rope □ Mallet □

Water container □ Lantern/torch □ Camping Gaz □

Matches □ Lighter □ Insect repellent □ Pans □ Money □

Portable shovel □ Plates □ Knives and forks □ Clothing □

Camping Knife □ Rucksack □ Food Items □ Mobile Phone □

Mobile phone charger □ Solar charger □ Map □ Pen □

Water Purifying tablets □ First Aid Kit □ Binoculars □

Location of nearest Town/Village:

_____

Mode of transport? Foot □ Bike □ Motorbike □ Car □

Location of landowner/farm:_____

Permission obtained to camp here? Y □ N □

Date: ____/____/_____

Expected Duration of stay? 1 □ 2 □ 3 □ 4 □ 5 □ Nights

How was the stay?_____

Any problems? _____

Notes:

Camping Equipment Check List

Tent □ Fly-sheet □ Tent poles □ Ground sheet □ Bed roll □
Sleeping bag □ Pillow □ Tent pegs □ Rope □ Mallet □
Water container □ Lantern/torch □ Camping Gaz □
Matches □ Lighter □ Insect repellent □ Pans □ Money □
Portable shovel □ Plates □ Knives and forks □ Clothing □
Camping Knife □ Rucksack □ Food Items □ Mobile Phone □
Mobile phone charger □ Solar charger □ Map □ Pen □
Water Purifying tablets □ First Aid Kit □ Binoculars □

Location of nearest Town/Village:

_____

Mode of transport? Foot □ Bike □ Motorbike □ Car □
Location of landowner/farm:_____
Permission obtained to camp here? Y □ N □
Date: ____/____/_____
Expected Duration of stay? 1 □ 2 □ 3 □ 4 □ 5 □ Nights
 How was the stay?_____
 Any problems? _____
Notes:

Camping Equipment Check List

Tent □ Fly-sheet □ Tent poles □ Ground sheet □ Bed roll □

Sleeping bag □ Pillow □ Tent pegs □ Rope □ Mallet □

Water container □ Lantern/torch □ Camping Gaz □

Matches □ Lighter □ Insect repellent □ Pans □ Money □

Portable shovel □ Plates □ Knives and forks □ Clothing □

Camping Knife □ Rucksack □ Food Items □ Mobile Phone □

Mobile phone charger □ Solar charger □ Map □ Pen □

Water Purifying tablets □ First Aid Kit □ Binoculars □

Location of nearest Town/Village:

_____

Mode of transport? Foot □ Bike □ Motorbike □ Car □

Location of landowner/farm:_____

Permission obtained to camp here? Y □ N □

Date: ____/____/_____

Expected Duration of stay? 1 □ 2 □ 3 □ 4 □ 5 □ Nights

 How was the stay?_____

 Any problems? _____

Notes:

Camping Equipment Check List

Tent □ Fly-sheet □ Tent poles □ Ground sheet □ Bed roll □
Sleeping bag □ Pillow □ Tent pegs □ Rope □ Mallet □
Water container □ Lantern/torch □ Camping Gaz □
Matches □ Lighter □ Insect repellent □ Pans □ Money □
Portable shovel □ Plates □ Knives and forks □ Clothing □
Camping Knife □ Rucksack □ Food Items □ Mobile Phone □
Mobile phone charger □ Solar charger □ Map □ Pen □
Water Purifying tablets □ First Aid Kit □ Binoculars □

Location of nearest Town/Village:

_____

Mode of transport? Foot □ Bike □ Motorbike □ Car □
Location of landowner/farm:_____
Permission obtained to camp here? Y □ N □
Date: _____/_____/_____
Expected Duration of stay? 1 □ 2 □ 3 □ 4 □ 5 □ Nights
How was the stay?_____
Any problems? _____
Notes:

Camping Equipment Check List

Tent □ Fly-sheet □ Tent poles □ Ground sheet □ Bed roll □

Sleeping bag □ Pillow □ Tent pegs □ Rope □ Mallet □

Water container □ Lantern/torch □ Camping Gaz □

Matches □ Lighter □ Insect repellent □ Pans □ Money □

Portable shovel □ Plates □ Knives and forks □ Clothing □

Camping Knife □ Rucksack □ Food Items □ Mobile Phone □

Mobile phone charger □ Solar charger □ Map □ Pen □

Water Purifying tablets □ First Aid Kit □ Binoculars □

Location of nearest Town/Village:

_____

Mode of transport? Foot □ Bike □ Motorbike □ Car □

Location of landowner/farm:_____

Permission obtained to camp here? Y □ N □

Date: ____/____/_____

Expected Duration of stay? 1 □ 2 □ 3 □ 4 □ 5 □ Nights

How was the stay?_____

Any problems? _____

Notes:

Camping Equipment Check List

Tent □ Fly-sheet □ Tent poles □ Ground sheet □ Bed roll □
Sleeping bag □ Pillow □ Tent pegs □ Rope □ Mallet □
Water container □ Lantern/torch □ Camping Gaz □
Matches □ Lighter □ Insect repellent □ Pans □ Money □
Portable shovel □ Plates □ Knives and forks □ Clothing □
Camping Knife □ Rucksack □ Food Items □ Mobile Phone □
Mobile phone charger □ Solar charger □ Map □ Pen □
Water Purifying tablets □ First Aid Kit □ Binoculars □

Location of nearest Town/Village:
_____

Mode of transport? Foot □ Bike □ Motorbike □ Car □
Location of landowner/farm:_____

Permission obtained to camp here? Y □ N □
Date: _____/_____/_____
Expected Duration of stay? 1 □ 2 □ 3 □ 4 □ 5 □ Nights
 How was the stay?_____
 Any problems? _____
Notes:

Camping Equipment Check List

Tent □ Fly-sheet □ Tent poles □ Ground sheet □ Bed roll □

Sleeping bag □ Pillow □ Tent pegs □ Rope □ Mallet □

Water container □ Lantern/torch □ Camping Gaz □

Matches □ Lighter □ Insect repellent □ Pans □ Money □

Portable shovel □ Plates □ Knives and forks □ Clothing □

Camping Knife □ Rucksack □ Food Items □ Mobile Phone □

Mobile phone charger □ Solar charger □ Map □ Pen □

Water Purifying tablets □ First Aid Kit □ Binoculars □

Location of nearest Town/Village:

_____

Mode of transport? Foot □ Bike □ Motorbike □ Car □

Location of landowner/farm:_____

Permission obtained to camp here? Y □ N □

Date: ____/____/_____

Expected Duration of stay? 1 □ 2 □ 3 □ 4 □ 5 □ Nights

 How was the stay?_____

 Any problems? _____

Notes:

Camping Equipment Check List

Tent □ Fly-sheet □ Tent poles □ Ground sheet □ Bed roll □
Sleeping bag □ Pillow □ Tent pegs □ Rope □ Mallet □
Water container □ Lantern/torch □ Camping Gaz □
Matches □ Lighter □ Insect repellent □ Pans □ Money □
Portable shovel □ Plates □ Knives and forks □ Clothing □
Camping Knife □ Rucksack □ Food Items □ Mobile Phone □
Mobile phone charger □ Solar charger □ Map □ Pen □
Water Purifying tablets □ First Aid Kit □ Binoculars □

Location of nearest Town/Village:
_____

Mode of transport? Foot □ Bike □ Motorbike □ Car □
Location of landowner/farm:_____
Permission obtained to camp here? Y □ N □
Date: ____/____/_____
Expected Duration of stay? 1 □ 2 □ 3 □ 4 □ 5 □ Nights
 How was the stay?_____
 Any problems? _____
Notes:

Camping Equipment Check List

Tent □ Fly-sheet □ Tent poles □ Ground sheet □ Bed roll □

Sleeping bag □ Pillow □ Tent pegs □ Rope □ Mallet □

Water container □ Lantern/torch □ Camping Gaz □

Matches □ Lighter □ Insect repellent □ Pans □ Money □

Portable shovel □ Plates □ Knives and forks □ Clothing □

Camping Knife □ Rucksack □ Food Items □ Mobile Phone □

Mobile phone charger □ Solar charger □ Map □ Pen □

Water Purifying tablets □ First Aid Kit □ Binoculars □

Location of nearest Town/Village:

_____

Mode of transport? Foot □ Bike □ Motorbike □ Car □

Location of landowner/farm:_____

Permission obtained to camp here? Y □ N □

Date: ____/____/_____

Expected Duration of stay? 1 □ 2 □ 3 □ 4 □ 5 □ Nights

 How was the stay?_____

 Any problems? _____

Notes:

Camping Equipment Check List

Tent □ Fly-sheet □ Tent poles □ Ground sheet □ Bed roll □

Sleeping bag □ Pillow □ Tent pegs □ Rope □ Mallet □

Water container □ Lantern/torch □ Camping Gaz □

Matches □ Lighter □ Insect repellent □ Pans □ Money □

Portable shovel □ Plates □ Knives and forks □ Clothing □

Camping Knife □ Rucksack □ Food Items □ Mobile Phone □

Mobile phone charger □ Solar charger □ Map □ Pen □

Water Purifying tablets □ First Aid Kit □ Binoculars □

Location of nearest Town/Village:

_____

Mode of transport? Foot □ Bike □ Motorbike □ Car □

Location of landowner/farm:_____

Permission obtained to camp here? Y □ N □

Date: _____/_____/_____

Expected Duration of stay? 1 □ 2 □ 3 □ 4 □ 5 □ Nights

 How was the stay?_____

 Any problems? _____

Notes:

Camping Equipment Check List

Tent □ Fly-sheet □ Tent poles □ Ground sheet □ Bed roll □

Sleeping bag □ Pillow □ Tent pegs □ Rope □ Mallet □

Water container □ Lantern/torch □ Camping Gaz □

Matches □ Lighter □ Insect repellent □ Pans □ Money □

Portable shovel □ Plates □ Knives and forks □ Clothing □

Camping Knife □ Rucksack □ Food Items □ Mobile Phone □

Mobile phone charger □ Solar charger □ Map □ Pen □

Water Purifying tablets □ First Aid Kit □ Binoculars □

Location of nearest Town/Village:

_____

Mode of transport? Foot □ Bike □ Motorbike □ Car □

Location of landowner/farm:_____

Permission obtained to camp here? Y □ N □

Date: _____/_____/_____

Expected Duration of stay? 1 □ 2 □ 3 □ 4 □ 5 □ Nights

How was the stay?_____

Any problems? _____

Notes:

Camping Equipment Check List

Tent □ Fly-sheet □ Tent poles □ Ground sheet □ Bed roll □
Sleeping bag □ Pillow □ Tent pegs □ Rope □ Mallet □
Water container □ Lantern/torch □ Camping Gaz □
Matches □ Lighter □ Insect repellent □ Pans □ Money □
Portable shovel □ Plates □ Knives and forks □ Clothing □
Camping Knife □ Rucksack □ Food Items □ Mobile Phone □
Mobile phone charger □ Solar charger □ Map □ Pen □
Water Purifying tablets □ First Aid Kit □ Binoculars □

Location of nearest Town/Village:

_____

Mode of transport? Foot □ Bike □ Motorbike □ Car □

Location of landowner/farm:_____

Permission obtained to camp here? Y □ N □

Date: ____/____/_____

Expected Duration of stay? 1 □ 2 □ 3 □ 4 □ 5 □ Nights

 How was the stay?_____

 Any problems? _____

Notes:

Camping Equipment Check List

Tent □ Fly-sheet □ Tent poles □ Ground sheet □ Bed roll □
Sleeping bag □ Pillow □ Tent pegs □ Rope □ Mallet □
Water container □ Lantern/torch □ Camping Gaz □
Matches □ Lighter □ Insect repellent □ Pans □ Money □
Portable shovel □ Plates □ Knives and forks □ Clothing □
Camping Knife □ Rucksack □ Food Items □ Mobile Phone □
Mobile phone charger □ Solar charger □ Map □ Pen □
Water Purifying tablets □ First Aid Kit □ Binoculars □

Location of nearest Town/Village:

_____

Mode of transport? Foot □ Bike □ Motorbike □ Car □

Location of landowner/farm:_____

Permission obtained to camp here? Y □ N □

Date: ____/____/_____

Expected Duration of stay? 1 □ 2 □ 3 □ 4 □ 5 □ Nights

How was the stay?_____

Any problems? _____

Notes:

Camping Equipment Check List

Tent □ Fly-sheet □ Tent poles □ Ground sheet □ Bed roll □
Sleeping bag □ Pillow □ Tent pegs □ Rope □ Mallet □
Water container □ Lantern/torch □ Camping Gaz □
Matches □ Lighter □ Insect repellent □ Pans □ Money □
Portable shovel □ Plates □ Knives and forks □ Clothing □
Camping Knife □ Rucksack □ Food Items □ Mobile Phone □
Mobile phone charger □ Solar charger □ Map □ Pen □
Water Purifying tablets □ First Aid Kit □ Binoculars □

Location of nearest Town/Village:

_____

Mode of transport? Foot □ Bike □ Motorbike □ Car □
Location of landowner/farm:_____
Permission obtained to camp here? Y □ N □
Date: ____/____/_____
Expected Duration of stay? 1 □ 2 □ 3 □ 4 □ 5 □ Nights
How was the stay?_____
Any problems? _____
Notes:

Camping Equipment Check List

Tent □ Fly-sheet □ Tent poles □ Ground sheet □ Bed roll □

Sleeping bag □ Pillow □ Tent pegs □ Rope □ Mallet □

Water container □ Lantern/torch □ Camping Gaz □

Matches □ Lighter □ Insect repellent □ Pans □ Money □

Portable shovel □ Plates □ Knives and forks □ Clothing □

Camping Knife □ Rucksack □ Food Items □ Mobile Phone □

Mobile phone charger □ Solar charger □ Map □ Pen □

Water Purifying tablets □ First Aid Kit □ Binoculars □

Location of nearest Town/Village:

_____

Mode of transport? Foot □ Bike □ Motorbike □ Car □

Location of landowner/farm:_____

Permission obtained to camp here? Y □ N □

Date: ____/____/_____

Expected Duration of stay? 1 □ 2 □ 3 □ 4 □ 5 □ Nights

How was the stay?_____

Any problems? _____

Notes:

Camping Equipment Check List

Tent □ Fly-sheet □ Tent poles □ Ground sheet □ Bed roll □

Sleeping bag □ Pillow □ Tent pegs □ Rope □ Mallet □

Water container □ Lantern/torch □ Camping Gaz □

Matches □ Lighter □ Insect repellent □ Pans □ Money □

Portable shovel □ Plates □ Knives and forks □ Clothing □

Camping Knife □ Rucksack □ Food Items □ Mobile Phone □

Mobile phone charger □ Solar charger □ Map □ Pen □

Water Purifying tablets □ First Aid Kit □ Binoculars □

Location of nearest Town/Village:

_____

Mode of transport? Foot □ Bike □ Motorbike □ Car □

Location of landowner/farm:_____

Permission obtained to camp here? Y □ N □

Date: ____/____/_____

Expected Duration of stay? 1 □ 2 □ 3 □ 4 □ 5 □ Nights

 How was the stay?_____

 Any problems? _____

Notes:

Camping Equipment Check List

Tent □ Fly-sheet □ Tent poles □ Ground sheet □ Bed roll □
Sleeping bag □ Pillow □ Tent pegs □ Rope □ Mallet □
Water container □ Lantern/torch □ Camping Gaz □
Matches □ Lighter □ Insect repellent □ Pans □ Money □
Portable shovel □ Plates □ Knives and forks □ Clothing □
Camping Knife □ Rucksack □ Food Items □ Mobile Phone □
Mobile phone charger □ Solar charger □ Map □ Pen □
Water Purifying tablets □ First Aid Kit □ Binoculars □

Location of nearest Town/Village:

_____

Mode of transport? Foot □ Bike □ Motorbike □ Car □
Location of landowner/farm:_____
Permission obtained to camp here? Y □ N □
Date: ____/____/_____
Expected Duration of stay? 1 □ 2 □ 3 □ 4 □ 5 □ Nights
 How was the stay?_____
 Any problems? _____
Notes:

Camping Equipment Check List

Tent □ Fly-sheet □ Tent poles □ Ground sheet □ Bed roll □
Sleeping bag □ Pillow □ Tent pegs □ Rope □ Mallet □
Water container □ Lantern/torch □ Camping Gaz □
Matches □ Lighter □ Insect repellent □ Pans □ Money □
Portable shovel □ Plates □ Knives and forks □ Clothing □
Camping Knife □ Rucksack □ Food Items □ Mobile Phone □
Mobile phone charger □ Solar charger □ Map □ Pen □
Water Purifying tablets □ First Aid Kit □ Binoculars □

Location of nearest Town/Village:

_____

Mode of transport? Foot □ Bike □ Motorbike □ Car □
Location of landowner/farm:_____
Permission obtained to camp here? Y □ N □
Date: ____/____/_____
Expected Duration of stay? 1 □ 2 □ 3 □ 4 □ 5 □ Nights
How was the stay?_____
Any problems? _____
Notes:

Camping Equipment Check List

Tent □ Fly-sheet □ Tent poles □ Ground sheet □ Bed roll □
Sleeping bag □ Pillow □ Tent pegs □ Rope □ Mallet □
Water container □ Lantern/torch □ Camping Gaz □
Matches □ Lighter □ Insect repellent □ Pans □ Money □
Portable shovel □ Plates □ Knives and forks □ Clothing □
Camping Knife □ Rucksack □ Food Items □ Mobile Phone □
Mobile phone charger □ Solar charger □ Map □ Pen □
Water Purifying tablets □ First Aid Kit □ Binoculars □

Location of nearest Town/Village:

_____

Mode of transport? Foot □ Bike □ Motorbike □ Car □

Location of landowner/farm:_____

Permission obtained to camp here? Y □ N □

Date: _____/_____/_____

Expected Duration of stay? 1 □ 2 □ 3 □ 4 □ 5 □ Nights

How was the stay?_____

Any problems? _____

Notes:

Camping Equipment Check List

Tent □ Fly-sheet □ Tent poles □ Ground sheet □ Bed roll □
Sleeping bag □ Pillow □ Tent pegs □ Rope □ Mallet □
Water container □ Lantern/torch □ Camping Gaz □
Matches □ Lighter □ Insect repellent □ Pans □ Money □
Portable shovel □ Plates □ Knives and forks □ Clothing □
Camping Knife □ Rucksack □ Food Items □ Mobile Phone □
Mobile phone charger □ Solar charger □ Map □ Pen □
Water Purifying tablets □ First Aid Kit □ Binoculars □

Location of nearest Town/Village:

_____

Mode of transport? Foot □ Bike □ Motorbike □ Car □
Location of landowner/farm:_____
Permission obtained to camp here? Y □ N □
Date: ____/____/_____
Expected Duration of stay? 1 □ 2 □ 3 □ 4 □ 5 □ Nights
 How was the stay?_____
 Any problems? _____
Notes:

Camping Equipment Check List

Tent □ Fly-sheet □ Tent poles □ Ground sheet □ Bed roll □
Sleeping bag □ Pillow □ Tent pegs □ Rope □ Mallet □
Water container □ Lantern/torch □ Camping Gaz □
Matches □ Lighter □ Insect repellent □ Pans □ Money □
Portable shovel □ Plates □ Knives and forks □ Clothing □
Camping Knife □ Rucksack □ Food Items □ Mobile Phone □
Mobile phone charger □ Solar charger □ Map □ Pen □
Water Purifying tablets □ First Aid Kit □ Binoculars □

Location of nearest Town/Village:

_____

Mode of transport? Foot □ Bike □ Motorbike □ Car □

Location of landowner/farm:_____

Permission obtained to camp here? Y □ N □

Date: ____/____/_____

Expected Duration of stay? 1 □ 2 □ 3 □ 4 □ 5 □ Nights

How was the stay?_____

Any problems? _____

Notes:

Camping Equipment Check List

Tent □ Fly-sheet □ Tent poles □ Ground sheet □ Bed roll □

Sleeping bag □ Pillow □ Tent pegs □ Rope □ Mallet □

Water container □ Lantern/torch □ Camping Gaz □

Matches □ Lighter □ Insect repellent □ Pans □ Money □

Portable shovel □ Plates □ Knives and forks □ Clothing □

Camping Knife □ Rucksack □ Food Items □ Mobile Phone □

Mobile phone charger □ Solar charger □ Map □ Pen □

Water Purifying tablets □ First Aid Kit □ Binoculars □

Location of nearest Town/Village:

_____

Mode of transport? Foot □ Bike □ Motorbike □ Car □

Location of landowner/farm:_____

Permission obtained to camp here? Y □ N □

Date: ____/____/_____

Expected Duration of stay? 1 □ 2 □ 3 □ 4 □ 5 □ Nights

 How was the stay?_____

 Any problems? _____

Notes:

Camping Equipment Check List

Tent □ Fly-sheet □ Tent poles □ Ground sheet □ Bed roll □

Sleeping bag □ Pillow □ Tent pegs □ Rope □ Mallet □

Water container □ Lantern/torch □ Camping Gaz □

Matches □ Lighter □ Insect repellent □ Pans □ Money □

Portable shovel □ Plates □ Knives and forks □ Clothing □

Camping Knife □ Rucksack □ Food Items □ Mobile Phone □

Mobile phone charger □ Solar charger □ Map □ Pen □

Water Purifying tablets □ First Aid Kit □ Binoculars □

Location of nearest Town/Village:

_____

Mode of transport? Foot □ Bike □ Motorbike □ Car □

Location of landowner/farm:_____

Permission obtained to camp here? Y □ N □

Date: ____/____/_____

Expected Duration of stay? 1 □ 2 □ 3 □ 4 □ 5 □ Nights

How was the stay?_____

Any problems? _____

Notes:

Camping Equipment Check List

Tent □ Fly-sheet □ Tent poles □ Ground sheet □ Bed roll □
Sleeping bag □ Pillow □ Tent pegs □ Rope □ Mallet □
Water container □ Lantern/torch □ Camping Gaz □
Matches □ Lighter □ Insect repellent □ Pans □ Money □
Portable shovel □ Plates □ Knives and forks □ Clothing □
Camping Knife □ Rucksack □ Food Items □ Mobile Phone □
Mobile phone charger □ Solar charger □ Map □ Pen □
Water Purifying tablets □ First Aid Kit □ Binoculars □

Location of nearest Town/Village:

_____

Mode of transport? Foot □ Bike □ Motorbike □ Car □
Location of landowner/farm:_____
Permission obtained to camp here? Y □ N □
Date: ____/____/_____
Expected Duration of stay? 1 □ 2 □ 3 □ 4 □ 5 □ Nights
 How was the stay?_____
 Any problems? _____
Notes:

Camping Equipment Check List

Tent □ Fly-sheet □ Tent poles □ Ground sheet □ Bed roll □
Sleeping bag □ Pillow □ Tent pegs □ Rope □ Mallet □
Water container □ Lantern/torch □ Camping Gaz □
Matches □ Lighter □ Insect repellent □ Pans □ Money □
Portable shovel □ Plates □ Knives and forks □ Clothing □
Camping Knife □ Rucksack □ Food Items □ Mobile Phone □
Mobile phone charger □ Solar charger □ Map □ Pen □
Water Purifying tablets □ First Aid Kit □ Binoculars □

Location of nearest Town/Village:
_____

Mode of transport? Foot □ Bike □ Motorbike □ Car □
Location of landowner/farm:_____
Permission obtained to camp here? Y □ N □
Date: ____/____/_____
Expected Duration of stay? 1 □ 2 □ 3 □ 4 □ 5 □ Nights
 How was the stay?_____
 Any problems? _____
Notes:

Camping Equipment Check List

Tent □ Fly-sheet □ Tent poles □ Ground sheet □ Bed roll □
Sleeping bag □ Pillow □ Tent pegs □ Rope □ Mallet □
Water container □ Lantern/torch □ Camping Gaz □
Matches □ Lighter □ Insect repellent □ Pans □ Money □
Portable shovel □ Plates □ Knives and forks □ Clothing □
Camping Knife □ Rucksack □ Food Items □ Mobile Phone □
Mobile phone charger □ Solar charger □ Map □ Pen □
Water Purifying tablets □ First Aid Kit □ Binoculars □

Location of nearest Town/Village:

_____

Mode of transport? Foot □ Bike □ Motorbike □ Car □
Location of landowner/farm: _____
Permission obtained to camp here? Y □ N □
Date: _____/_____/_____
Expected Duration of stay? 1 □ 2 □ 3 □ 4 □ 5 □ Nights
 How was the stay? _____
 Any problems? _____
Notes:

Camping Equipment Check List

Tent □ Fly-sheet □ Tent poles □ Ground sheet □ Bed roll □

Sleeping bag □ Pillow □ Tent pegs □ Rope □ Mallet □

Water container □ Lantern/torch □ Camping Gaz □

Matches □ Lighter □ Insect repellent □ Pans □ Money □

Portable shovel □ Plates □ Knives and forks □ Clothing □

Camping Knife □ Rucksack □ Food Items □ Mobile Phone □

Mobile phone charger □ Solar charger □ Map □ Pen □

Water Purifying tablets □ First Aid Kit □ Binoculars □

Location of nearest Town/Village:

_____

Mode of transport? Foot □ Bike □ Motorbike □ Car □

Location of landowner/farm:_____

Permission obtained to camp here? Y □ N □

Date: _____/_____/_____

Expected Duration of stay? 1 □ 2 □ 3 □ 4 □ 5 □ Nights

 How was the stay?_____

 Any problems? _____

Notes:

Camping Equipment Check List

Tent □ Fly-sheet □ Tent poles □ Ground sheet □ Bed roll □
Sleeping bag □ Pillow □ Tent pegs □ Rope □ Mallet □
Water container □ Lantern/torch □ Camping Gaz □
Matches □ Lighter □ Insect repellent □ Pans □ Money □
Portable shovel □ Plates □ Knives and forks □ Clothing □
Camping Knife □ Rucksack □ Food Items □ Mobile Phone □
Mobile phone charger □ Solar charger □ Map □ Pen □
Water Purifying tablets □ First Aid Kit □ Binoculars □

Location of nearest Town/Village:

_____

Mode of transport? Foot □ Bike □ Motorbike □ Car □
Location of landowner/farm:_____
Permission obtained to camp here? Y □ N □
Date: ____/____/_____
Expected Duration of stay? 1 □ 2 □ 3 □ 4 □ 5 □ Nights
 How was the stay?_____
 Any problems? _____
Notes:

Camping Equipment Check List

Tent □ Fly-sheet □ Tent poles □ Ground sheet □ Bed roll □
Sleeping bag □ Pillow □ Tent pegs □ Rope □ Mallet □
Water container □ Lantern/torch □ Camping Gaz □
Matches □ Lighter □ Insect repellent □ Pans □ Money □
Portable shovel □ Plates □ Knives and forks □ Clothing □
Camping Knife □ Rucksack □ Food Items □ Mobile Phone □
Mobile phone charger □ Solar charger □ Map □ Pen □
Water Purifying tablets □ First Aid Kit □ Binoculars □

Location of nearest Town/Village:
_____

Mode of transport? Foot □ Bike □ Motorbike □ Car □
Location of landowner/farm:_____
Permission obtained to camp here? Y □ N □
Date: ____/____/_____
Expected Duration of stay? 1 □ 2 □ 3 □ 4 □ 5 □ Nights
How was the stay?_____
Any problems? _____
Notes:

Camping Equipment Check List

Tent □ Fly-sheet □ Tent poles □ Ground sheet □ Bed roll □

Sleeping bag □ Pillow □ Tent pegs □ Rope □ Mallet □

Water container □ Lantern/torch □ Camping Gaz □

Matches □ Lighter □ Insect repellent □ Pans □ Money □

Portable shovel □ Plates □ Knives and forks □ Clothing □

Camping Knife □ Rucksack □ Food Items □ Mobile Phone □

Mobile phone charger □ Solar charger □ Map □ Pen □

Water Purifying tablets □ First Aid Kit □ Binoculars □

Location of nearest Town/Village:

_____

Mode of transport? Foot □ Bike □ Motorbike □ Car □

Location of landowner/farm:_____

Permission obtained to camp here? Y □ N □

Date: ____/____/_____

Expected Duration of stay? 1 □ 2 □ 3 □ 4 □ 5 □ Nights

 How was the stay?_____

 Any problems? _____

Notes:

Camping Equipment Check List

Tent □ Fly-sheet □ Tent poles □ Ground sheet □ Bed roll □

Sleeping bag □ Pillow □ Tent pegs □ Rope □ Mallet □

Water container □ Lantern/torch □ Camping Gaz □

Matches □ Lighter □ Insect repellent □ Pans □ Money □

Portable shovel □ Plates □ Knives and forks □ Clothing □

Camping Knife □ Rucksack □ Food Items □ Mobile Phone □

Mobile phone charger □ Solar charger □ Map □ Pen □

Water Purifying tablets □ First Aid Kit □ Binoculars □

Location of nearest Town/Village:

_____

Mode of transport? Foot □ Bike □ Motorbike □ Car □

Location of landowner/farm:_____

Permission obtained to camp here? Y □ N □

Date: ____/____/_____

Expected Duration of stay? 1 □ 2 □ 3 □ 4 □ 5 □ Nights

How was the stay?_____

Any problems? _____

Notes:

Camping Equipment Check List

Tent □ Fly-sheet □ Tent poles □ Ground sheet □ Bed roll □
Sleeping bag □ Pillow □ Tent pegs □ Rope □ Mallet □
Water container □ Lantern/torch □ Camping Gaz □
Matches □ Lighter □ Insect repellent □ Pans □ Money □
Portable shovel □ Plates □ Knives and forks □ Clothing □
Camping Knife □ Rucksack □ Food Items □ Mobile Phone □
Mobile phone charger □ Solar charger □ Map □ Pen □
Water Purifying tablets □ First Aid Kit □ Binoculars □

Location of nearest Town/Village:
_____

Mode of transport? Foot □ Bike □ Motorbike □ Car □
Location of landowner/farm:_____
Permission obtained to camp here? Y □ N □
Date: ____/____/_____
Expected Duration of stay? 1 □ 2 □ 3 □ 4 □ 5 □ Nights
How was the stay?_____
Any problems? _____
Notes:

Camping Equipment Check List

Tent □ Fly-sheet □ Tent poles □ Ground sheet □ Bed roll □

Sleeping bag □ Pillow □ Tent pegs □ Rope □ Mallet □

Water container □ Lantern/torch □ Camping Gaz □

Matches □ Lighter □ Insect repellent □ Pans □ Money □

Portable shovel □ Plates □ Knives and forks □ Clothing □

Camping Knife □ Rucksack □ Food Items □ Mobile Phone □

Mobile phone charger □ Solar charger □ Map □ Pen □

Water Purifying tablets □ First Aid Kit □ Binoculars □

Location of nearest Town/Village:

_____

Mode of transport? Foot □ Bike □ Motorbike □ Car □

Location of landowner/farm:_____

Permission obtained to camp here? Y □ N □

Date: ____/____/_____

Expected Duration of stay? 1 □ 2 □ 3 □ 4 □ 5 □ Nights

How was the stay?_____

Any problems? _____

Notes:

Camping Equipment Check List

Tent □ Fly-sheet □ Tent poles □ Ground sheet □ Bed roll □

Sleeping bag □ Pillow □ Tent pegs □ Rope □ Mallet □

Water container □ Lantern/torch □ Camping Gaz □

Matches □ Lighter □ Insect repellent □ Pans □ Money □

Portable shovel □ Plates □ Knives and forks □ Clothing □

Camping Knife □ Rucksack □ Food Items □ Mobile Phone □

Mobile phone charger □ Solar charger □ Map □ Pen □

Water Purifying tablets □ First Aid Kit □ Binoculars □

Location of nearest Town/Village:

_____

Mode of transport? Foot □ Bike □ Motorbike □ Car □

Location of landowner/farm:_____

Permission obtained to camp here? Y □ N □

Date: ____/____/_____

Expected Duration of stay? 1 □ 2 □ 3 □ 4 □ 5 □ Nights

 How was the stay?_____

 Any problems? _____

Notes:

Camping Equipment Check List

Tent □ Fly-sheet □ Tent poles □ Ground sheet □ Bed roll □

Sleeping bag □ Pillow □ Tent pegs □ Rope □ Mallet □

Water container □ Lantern/torch □ Camping Gaz □

Matches □ Lighter □ Insect repellent □ Pans □ Money □

Portable shovel □ Plates □ Knives and forks □ Clothing □

Camping Knife □ Rucksack □ Food Items □ Mobile Phone □

Mobile phone charger □ Solar charger □ Map □ Pen □

Water Purifying tablets □ First Aid Kit □ Binoculars □

Location of nearest Town/Village:

_____

Mode of transport? Foot □ Bike □ Motorbike □ Car □

Location of landowner/farm:_____

Permission obtained to camp here? Y □ N □

Date: ____/____/_____

Expected Duration of stay? 1 □ 2 □ 3 □ 4 □ 5 □ Nights

How was the stay?_____

Any problems? _____

Notes:

Camping Equipment Check List

Tent □ Fly-sheet □ Tent poles □ Ground sheet □ Bed roll □
Sleeping bag □ Pillow □ Tent pegs □ Rope □ Mallet □
Water container □ Lantern/torch □ Camping Gaz □
Matches □ Lighter □ Insect repellent □ Pans □ Money □
Portable shovel □ Plates □ Knives and forks □ Clothing □
Camping Knife □ Rucksack □ Food Items □ Mobile Phone □
Mobile phone charger □ Solar charger □ Map □ Pen □
Water Purifying tablets □ First Aid Kit □ Binoculars □

Location of nearest Town/Village:

_____

Mode of transport? Foot □ Bike □ Motorbike □ Car □

Location of landowner/farm:_____

Permission obtained to camp here? Y □ N □

Date: ____/____/_____

Expected Duration of stay? 1 □ 2 □ 3 □ 4 □ 5 □ Nights

How was the stay?_____

Any problems? _____

Notes:

Camping Equipment Check List

Tent ☐ Fly-sheet ☐ Tent poles ☐ Ground sheet ☐ Bed roll ☐

Sleeping bag ☐ Pillow ☐ Tent pegs ☐ Rope ☐ Mallet ☐

Water container ☐ Lantern/torch ☐ Camping Gaz ☐

Matches ☐ Lighter ☐ Insect repellent ☐ Pans ☐ Money ☐

Portable shovel ☐ Plates ☐ Knives and forks ☐ Clothing ☐

Camping Knife ☐ Rucksack ☐ Food Items ☐ Mobile Phone ☐

Mobile phone charger ☐ Solar charger ☐ Map ☐ Pen ☐

Water Purifying tablets ☐ First Aid Kit ☐ Binoculars ☐

Location of nearest Town/Village:

_____

Mode of transport? Foot ☐ Bike ☐ Motorbike ☐ Car ☐

Location of landowner/farm:_____

Permission obtained to camp here? Y ☐ N ☐

Date: ____/____/_____

Expected Duration of stay? 1 ☐ 2 ☐ 3 ☐ 4 ☐ 5 ☐ Nights

 How was the stay?_____

 Any problems? _____

Notes:

Camping Equipment Check List

Tent □ Fly-sheet □ Tent poles □ Ground sheet □ Bed roll □
Sleeping bag □ Pillow □ Tent pegs □ Rope □ Mallet □
Water container □ Lantern/torch □ Camping Gaz □
Matches □ Lighter □ Insect repellent □ Pans □ Money □
Portable shovel □ Plates □ Knives and forks □ Clothing □
Camping Knife □ Rucksack □ Food Items □ Mobile Phone □
Mobile phone charger □ Solar charger □ Map □ Pen □
Water Purifying tablets □ First Aid Kit □ Binoculars □

Location of nearest Town/Village:

_____

Mode of transport? Foot □ Bike □ Motorbike □ Car □
Location of landowner/farm:_____
Permission obtained to camp here? Y □ N □
Date: _____/_____/_____
Expected Duration of stay? 1 □ 2 □ 3 □ 4 □ 5 □ Nights
How was the stay?_____
Any problems? _____
Notes:

Camping Equipment Check List

Tent □ Fly-sheet □ Tent poles □ Ground sheet □ Bed roll □

Sleeping bag □ Pillow □ Tent pegs □ Rope □ Mallet □

Water container □ Lantern/torch □ Camping Gaz □

Matches □ Lighter □ Insect repellent □ Pans □ Money □

Portable shovel □ Plates □ Knives and forks □ Clothing □

Camping Knife □ Rucksack □ Food Items □ Mobile Phone □

Mobile phone charger □ Solar charger □ Map □ Pen □

Water Purifying tablets □ First Aid Kit □ Binoculars □

Location of nearest Town/Village:

_____

Mode of transport? Foot □ Bike □ Motorbike □ Car □

Location of landowner/farm:_____

Permission obtained to camp here? Y □ N □

Date: ____/____/_____

Expected Duration of stay? 1 □ 2 □ 3 □ 4 □ 5 □ Nights

 How was the stay?_____

 Any problems? _____

Notes:

Camping Equipment Check List

Tent □ Fly-sheet □ Tent poles □ Ground sheet □ Bed roll □
Sleeping bag □ Pillow □ Tent pegs □ Rope □ Mallet □
Water container □ Lantern/torch □ Camping Gaz □
Matches □ Lighter □ Insect repellent □ Pans □ Money □
Portable shovel □ Plates □ Knives and forks □ Clothing □
Camping Knife □ Rucksack □ Food Items □ Mobile Phone □
Mobile phone charger □ Solar charger □ Map □ Pen □
Water Purifying tablets □ First Aid Kit □ Binoculars □

Location of nearest Town/Village:

_____

Mode of transport? Foot □ Bike □ Motorbike □ Car □
Location of landowner/farm:_____
Permission obtained to camp here? Y □ N □
Date: ____/____/_____
Expected Duration of stay? 1 □ 2 □ 3 □ 4 □ 5 □ Nights
 How was the stay?_____
 Any problems? _____
Notes:

Camping Equipment Check List

Tent □ Fly-sheet □ Tent poles □ Ground sheet □ Bed roll □
Sleeping bag □ Pillow □ Tent pegs □ Rope □ Mallet □
Water container □ Lantern/torch □ Camping Gaz □
Matches □ Lighter □ Insect repellent □ Pans □ Money □
Portable shovel □ Plates □ Knives and forks □ Clothing □
Camping Knife □ Rucksack □ Food Items □ Mobile Phone □
Mobile phone charger □ Solar charger □ Map □ Pen □
Water Purifying tablets □ First Aid Kit □ Binoculars □

Location of nearest Town/Village:
_____

Mode of transport? Foot □ Bike □ Motorbike □ Car □
Location of landowner/farm:_____
Permission obtained to camp here? Y □ N □
Date: ____/____/_____
Expected Duration of stay? 1 □ 2 □ 3 □ 4 □ 5 □ Nights
 How was the stay?_____
 Any problems? _____
Notes:

Camping Equipment Check List

Tent □ Fly-sheet □ Tent poles □ Ground sheet □ Bed roll □
Sleeping bag □ Pillow □ Tent pegs □ Rope □ Mallet □
Water container □ Lantern/torch □ Camping Gaz □
Matches □ Lighter □ Insect repellent □ Pans □ Money □
Portable shovel □ Plates □ Knives and forks □ Clothing □
Camping Knife □ Rucksack □ Food Items □ Mobile Phone □
Mobile phone charger □ Solar charger □ Map □ Pen □
Water Purifying tablets □ First Aid Kit □ Binoculars □

Location of nearest Town/Village:

_____

Mode of transport? Foot □ Bike □ Motorbike □ Car □

Location of landowner/farm:_____

Permission obtained to camp here? Y □ N □

Date: ____/____/_____

Expected Duration of stay? 1 □ 2 □ 3 □ 4 □ 5 □ Nights

How was the stay?_____

Any problems? _____

Notes:

Camping Equipment Check List

Tent □ Fly-sheet □ Tent poles □ Ground sheet □ Bed roll □

Sleeping bag □ Pillow □ Tent pegs □ Rope □ Mallet □

Water container □ Lantern/torch □ Camping Gaz □

Matches □ Lighter □ Insect repellent □ Pans □ Money □

Portable shovel □ Plates □ Knives and forks □ Clothing □

Camping Knife □ Rucksack □ Food Items □ Mobile Phone □

Mobile phone charger □ Solar charger □ Map □ Pen □

Water Purifying tablets □ First Aid Kit □ Binoculars □

Location of nearest Town/Village:

_____

Mode of transport? Foot □ Bike □ Motorbike □ Car □

Location of landowner/farm:_____

Permission obtained to camp here? Y □ N □

Date: _____/_____/_____

Expected Duration of stay? 1 □ 2 □ 3 □ 4 □ 5 □ Nights

How was the stay?_____

Any problems? _____

Notes:

Camping Equipment Check List

Tent □ Fly-sheet □ Tent poles □ Ground sheet □ Bed roll □
Sleeping bag □ Pillow □ Tent pegs □ Rope □ Mallet □
Water container □ Lantern/torch □ Camping Gaz □
Matches □ Lighter □ Insect repellent □ Pans □ Money □
Portable shovel □ Plates □ Knives and forks □ Clothing □
Camping Knife □ Rucksack □ Food Items □ Mobile Phone □
Mobile phone charger □ Solar charger □ Map □ Pen □
Water Purifying tablets □ First Aid Kit □ Binoculars □

Location of nearest Town/Village:

_____

Mode of transport? Foot □ Bike □ Motorbike □ Car □

Location of landowner/farm:_____

Permission obtained to camp here? Y □ N □

Date: ____/____/_____

Expected Duration of stay? 1 □ 2 □ 3 □ 4 □ 5 □ Nights

How was the stay?_____

Any problems? _____

Notes:

Camping Equipment Check List

Tent □ Fly-sheet □ Tent poles □ Ground sheet □ Bed roll □
Sleeping bag □ Pillow □ Tent pegs □ Rope □ Mallet □
Water container □ Lantern/torch □ Camping Gaz □
Matches □ Lighter □ Insect repellent □ Pans □ Money □
Portable shovel □ Plates □ Knives and forks □ Clothing □
Camping Knife □ Rucksack □ Food Items □ Mobile Phone □
Mobile phone charger □ Solar charger □ Map □ Pen □
Water Purifying tablets □ First Aid Kit □ Binoculars □

Location of nearest Town/Village:
_____

Mode of transport? Foot □ Bike □ Motorbike □ Car □
Location of landowner/farm:_____
Permission obtained to camp here? Y □ N □
Date: ____/____/_____
Expected Duration of stay? 1 □ 2 □ 3 □ 4 □ 5 □ Nights
 How was the stay?_____
 Any problems? _____
Notes:

Camping Equipment Check List

Tent □ Fly-sheet □ Tent poles □ Ground sheet □ Bed roll □

Sleeping bag □ Pillow □ Tent pegs □ Rope □ Mallet □

Water container □ Lantern/torch □ Camping Gaz □

Matches □ Lighter □ Insect repellent □ Pans □ Money □

Portable shovel □ Plates □ Knives and forks □ Clothing □

Camping Knife □ Rucksack □ Food Items □ Mobile Phone □

Mobile phone charger □ Solar charger □ Map □ Pen □

Water Purifying tablets □ First Aid Kit □ Binoculars □

Location of nearest Town/Village:

_____

Mode of transport? Foot □ Bike □ Motorbike □ Car □

Location of landowner/farm:_____

Permission obtained to camp here? Y □ N □

Date: ____/____/_____

Expected Duration of stay? 1 □ 2 □ 3 □ 4 □ 5 □ Nights

 How was the stay?_____

 Any problems? _____

Notes:

Camping Equipment Check List

Tent □ Fly-sheet □ Tent poles □ Ground sheet □ Bed roll □
Sleeping bag □ Pillow □ Tent pegs □ Rope □ Mallet □
Water container □ Lantern/torch □ Camping Gaz □
Matches □ Lighter □ Insect repellent □ Pans □ Money □
Portable shovel □ Plates □ Knives and forks □ Clothing □
Camping Knife □ Rucksack □ Food Items □ Mobile Phone □
Mobile phone charger □ Solar charger □ Map □ Pen □
Water Purifying tablets □ First Aid Kit □ Binoculars □

Location of nearest Town/Village:

_____

Mode of transport? Foot □ Bike □ Motorbike □ Car □
Location of landowner/farm:_____
Permission obtained to camp here? Y □ N □
Date: ____/____/_____
Expected Duration of stay? 1 □ 2 □ 3 □ 4 □ 5 □ Nights
 How was the stay?_____
 Any problems? _____
Notes:

Camping Equipment Check List

Tent □ Fly-sheet □ Tent poles □ Ground sheet □ Bed roll □
Sleeping bag □ Pillow □ Tent pegs □ Rope □ Mallet □
Water container □ Lantern/torch □ Camping Gaz □
Matches □ Lighter □ Insect repellent □ Pans □ Money □
Portable shovel □ Plates □ Knives and forks □ Clothing □
Camping Knife □ Rucksack □ Food Items □ Mobile Phone □
Mobile phone charger □ Solar charger □ Map □ Pen □
Water Purifying tablets □ First Aid Kit □ Binoculars □

Location of nearest Town/Village:

_____

Mode of transport? Foot □ Bike □ Motorbike □ Car □

Location of landowner/farm:_____

Permission obtained to camp here? Y □ N □

Date: ____/____/_____

Expected Duration of stay? 1 □ 2 □ 3 □ 4 □ 5 □ Nights

 How was the stay?_____

 Any problems? _____

Notes:

Camping Equipment Check List

Tent □ Fly-sheet □ Tent poles □ Ground sheet □ Bed roll □

Sleeping bag □ Pillow □ Tent pegs □ Rope □ Mallet □

Water container □ Lantern/torch □ Camping Gaz □

Matches □ Lighter □ Insect repellent □ Pans □ Money □

Portable shovel □ Plates □ Knives and forks □ Clothing □

Camping Knife □ Rucksack □ Food Items □ Mobile Phone □

Mobile phone charger □ Solar charger □ Map □ Pen □

Water Purifying tablets □ First Aid Kit □ Binoculars □

Location of nearest Town/Village:

_____

Mode of transport? Foot □ Bike □ Motorbike □ Car □

Location of landowner/farm: _____

Permission obtained to camp here? Y □ N □

Date: ____/____/_____

Expected Duration of stay? 1 □ 2 □ 3 □ 4 □ 5 □ Nights

How was the stay? _____

Any problems? _____

Notes:

Camping Equipment Check List

Tent □ Fly-sheet □ Tent poles □ Ground sheet □ Bed roll □
Sleeping bag □ Pillow □ Tent pegs □ Rope □ Mallet □
Water container □ Lantern/torch □ Camping Gaz □
Matches □ Lighter □ Insect repellent □ Pans □ Money □
Portable shovel □ Plates □ Knives and forks □ Clothing □
Camping Knife □ Rucksack □ Food Items □ Mobile Phone □
Mobile phone charger □ Solar charger □ Map □ Pen □
Water Purifying tablets □ First Aid Kit □ Binoculars □

Location of nearest Town/Village:

_____

Mode of transport? Foot □ Bike □ Motorbike □ Car □

Location of landowner/farm:_____

Permission obtained to camp here? Y □ N □

Date: ____/____/_____

Expected Duration of stay? 1 □ 2 □ 3 □ 4 □ 5 □ Nights

How was the stay?_____

Any problems? _____

Notes:

Camping Equipment Check List

Tent □ Fly-sheet □ Tent poles □ Ground sheet □ Bed roll □

Sleeping bag □ Pillow □ Tent pegs □ Rope □ Mallet □

Water container □ Lantern/torch □ Camping Gaz □

Matches □ Lighter □ Insect repellent □ Pans □ Money □

Portable shovel □ Plates □ Knives and forks □ Clothing □

Camping Knife □ Rucksack □ Food Items □ Mobile Phone □

Mobile phone charger □ Solar charger □ Map □ Pen □

Water Purifying tablets □ First Aid Kit □ Binoculars □

Location of nearest Town/Village:

_____

Mode of transport? Foot □ Bike □ Motorbike □ Car □

Location of landowner/farm:_____

Permission obtained to camp here? Y □ N □

Date: ____/____/_____

Expected Duration of stay? 1 □ 2 □ 3 □ 4 □ 5 □ Nights

 How was the stay?_____

 Any problems? _____

Notes:

Camping Equipment Check List

Tent □ Fly-sheet □ Tent poles □ Ground sheet □ Bed roll □

Sleeping bag □ Pillow □ Tent pegs □ Rope □ Mallet □

Water container □ Lantern/torch □ Camping Gaz □

Matches □ Lighter □ Insect repellent □ Pans □ Money □

Portable shovel □ Plates □ Knives and forks □ Clothing □

Camping Knife □ Rucksack □ Food Items □ Mobile Phone □

Mobile phone charger □ Solar charger □ Map □ Pen □

Water Purifying tablets □ First Aid Kit □ Binoculars □

Location of nearest Town/Village:

_____

Mode of transport? Foot □ Bike □ Motorbike □ Car □

Location of landowner/farm:_____

Permission obtained to camp here? Y □ N □

Date: ____/____/_____

Expected Duration of stay? 1 □ 2 □ 3 □ 4 □ 5 □ Nights

 How was the stay?_____

 Any problems? _____

Notes:

Camping Equipment Check List

Tent ☐ Fly-sheet ☐ Tent poles ☐ Ground sheet ☐ Bed roll ☐
Sleeping bag ☐ Pillow ☐ Tent pegs ☐ Rope ☐ Mallet ☐
Water container ☐ Lantern/torch ☐ Camping Gaz ☐
Matches ☐ Lighter ☐ Insect repellent ☐ Pans ☐ Money ☐
Portable shovel ☐ Plates ☐ Knives and forks ☐ Clothing ☐
Camping Knife ☐ Rucksack ☐ Food Items ☐ Mobile Phone ☐
Mobile phone charger ☐ Solar charger ☐ Map ☐ Pen ☐
Water Purifying tablets ☐ First Aid Kit ☐ Binoculars ☐

Location of nearest Town/Village:

_____

Mode of transport? Foot ☐ Bike ☐ Motorbike ☐ Car ☐
Location of landowner/farm:_____
Permission obtained to camp here? Y ☐ N ☐
Date: _____/_____/_____
Expected Duration of stay? 1 ☐ 2 ☐ 3 ☐ 4 ☐ 5 ☐ Nights
 How was the stay?_____
 Any problems? _____
Notes:

Camping Equipment Check List

Tent □ Fly-sheet □ Tent poles □ Ground sheet □ Bed roll □

Sleeping bag □ Pillow □ Tent pegs □ Rope □ Mallet □

Water container □ Lantern/torch □ Camping Gaz □

Matches □ Lighter □ Insect repellent □ Pans □ Money □

Portable shovel □ Plates □ Knives and forks □ Clothing □

Camping Knife □ Rucksack □ Food Items □ Mobile Phone □

Mobile phone charger □ Solar charger □ Map □ Pen □

Water Purifying tablets □ First Aid Kit □ Binoculars □

Location of nearest Town/Village:

_____

Mode of transport? Foot □ Bike □ Motorbike □ Car □

Location of landowner/farm:_____

Permission obtained to camp here? Y □ N □

Date: ____/____/_____

Expected Duration of stay? 1 □ 2 □ 3 □ 4 □ 5 □ Nights

 How was the stay?_____

 Any problems? _____

Notes:

Final Notes / Thoughts on wild camping: